To My dearest

with all my love.

Henry, April 1993.

THE IT CHALLENGE
IT and strategy in financial services

BUSINESS INFORMATION TECHNOLOGY SERIES

THE IT CHALLENGE
IT and strategy in financial services

Edited by

HARRY SCARBROUGH

Prentice Hall

New York   London   Toronto   Sydney   Tokyo   Singapore

First published 1992 by
Prentice Hall International (UK) Ltd
Campus 400, Maylands Avenue
Hemel Hempstead
Hertfordshire, HP2 7EZ
A division of
Simon & Schuster International Group

Typeset in 10/12 pt Palatino
by Keyset Composition

Printed and bound in Great Britain at
the University Press Cambridge

Library of Congress Cataloging-in-Publication Data

The IT challenge: IT and strategy in financial services/Harry
    Scarbrough, editor.
        p. cm. — (Business information technology series)
    Includes bibliographical references and index.
    ISBN 0-13-493420-2 : $29.99
        1. Financial services industry—Data processing.   2. Information
    technology.   I. Scarbrough, Harry, 1955–   II. Series.
    HG173.I845   1992   92-8203
    332.1′0285—dc20   CIP

British Library Cataloguing in Publication Data

A catalogue record for this book is available from
the British Library

ISBN 0-13-493420-2 (hbk)

---

1 2 3 4 5   96   95   94   93   92

Contents

List of tables

List of figures

Chapter 1

Introduction

Harry Scarbrough

Most of the issues that provoke deep managerial concern are short-term and cyclical. They include the business cycle and the immediate prospects for boom or recession. They may also encompass the annual cycles of financial reporting and management control. But in the retail financial services sector, there is one issue whose importance transcends the usual market and management cycles. This is the increasingly pervasive application of IT (information technology) which is creating long-run and inexorable waves of change in financial services. The application of IT poses a strategic challenge to all firms in the sector.

This book addresses the scale and nature of that challenge in three ways. First, it analyses the market context in which IT is deployed. Secondly, it reviews the business opportunities created by IT. And thirdly, it considers the way in which IT is managed and where companies could improve. The emphasis throughout is less upon the generalised impact of IT than upon its role in delivering products, enhancing skills and supporting strategies.

This focus on the management of IT drives the book towards the concerns of general managers. For this group, and for those analysts and academics associated with the sector, an awareness of IT applications is becoming a critical element of strategic thinking. The traditional professional skills of general management – be they in banking, actuarialism or building society management – are no longer enough. Moreover, as the sector changes, IT awareness needs be linked to a sectoral perspective which transcends the immediate competitive environment. It is axiomatic to the aims of this book that in expanding their awareness of IT's potential, management need to view this new technology through a predominantly sectoral perspective.

As a first step towards explaining why IT is so important to financial services, we could simply note that the sector is one of the biggest users of IT. Financial services is a highly information-intensive sector, and massive

1

amounts are invested in the processing and manipulation of information; IT investments in a major UK bank could easily exceed a billion pounds over a five-year period. The sector also has greater experience of using computer technology than any other industrial sector. Within every major financial services firm, large IT divisions or departments have evolved to guide and control technological development.

Yet, despite the scale of investment and the length of experience, IT has become a critical problem for management in financial services. In fact, with large investments in IT producing what are sometimes seen as meagre returns, top management dissatisfaction seems to be growing rather than diminishing.

The reasons for the increasing management concern with IT are manifold. One useful way of understanding it is through the level of *uncertainty* associated with the application of IT. In part, such uncertainty is a distinctive feature of the technology itself. The potential of IT – that is, our knowledge of what it could do – continues to outstrip actual applications. This gap between potential and application is a constant stimulus to innovations, generated both from within the sector and from an extensive IT supply industry which has a vested interest in maintaining the turnover in technological investments. The pattern of innovations in the recent period is surveyed in Chapter 4, which includes a look at customer databases, home banking and expert systems. Such innovations have important competitive implications and help to foster uncertainty about the kinds of product and system needed to maintain or expand the market positions of financial services providers.

Just as significant a source of uncertainty is the sector itself. As we describe in Chapter 2, the uncertainty created by a turbulent business environment stimulates a high level of strategic activity of which technology is but one dimension. Where a more stable environment promotes the use of technology to increase the efficiency of existing processes, this kind of uncertainty encourages innovations and IT use aimed at competitive advantage. The increasing proliferation of IT-based innovations in both the UK and the USA is surveyed – the latter in Chapter 6 – and the consequences for competition analysed. One important lesson from this survey is that, whether financial service firms invest in IT for offensive or, more commonly, defensive reasons, the overall effect is further to increase business uncertainty while raising the stakes for other players.

Finally, as well as the external competitive uncertainty, there remains critical uncertainty about the internal management of IT within organisations. As we note in Chapter 7, attempts to link IT use to strategy are often dogged by the problems and uncertainties associated with managing organisational change and controlling the IT function.

STRUCTURE OF THE BOOK

This book will explore the key uncertainties facing the financial services sector, providing an overview of what we see as the most critical issues in the management of IT. In terms of coverage, the book deals with the major industrial groupings within the sector – banking, building societies and insurance. In order to provide all-round coverage of this complex and increasingly global industry, chapters have been commissioned from authors with specific expertise on the use of IT in different technical and product-market areas of financial services, both in the UK and internationally.

The book has been assembled and organised in such a way as to provide an up-to-date, *analytical* view of IT and strategy in the sector, and not simply a descriptive review of current events. This aim is reflected in the breakdown of the chapters, focusing on the key issues facing the UK sector and also drawing on international data to illuminate possible trends and management issues.

Chapter 2 surveys the evolution of the sector and its implications for IT through an analysis of the current positions of the major players and trends in competition. It highlights the implications of such factors for the development of IT.

Chapter 3 examines the interaction between the potential of IT and the structural features of financial services. It highlights the importance of such features in the the use of IT for product and infrastructural development. The development of home and office services provides an example of the issues which IT-based systems pose for management.

Chapter 4 by Dr Rob Procter deals with some of the most salient technological trends in the corporate use of IT, specifically: database technology; distributed IT; decision support and expert systems; and the integration of computing and communications. It not only analyses the organisational implications of these technological developments, but also addresses the kind of user and customer interface needed to make IT effective in a business context.

Chapter 5 by Steve Worthington tackles one of the most unpredictable long-term issues facing the UK sector. This is the question of possible moves by retail groups into financial services. This has been highlighted by the successful application of Marks and Spencer's retail skills to the marketing of personal loans and unit trusts. The inability of the large financial institutions to emulate such skills is evidence enough of the potential opportunities available to retailers. And developments in EFTPOS (electronic funds transfer at point of sale), credit cards, personal loans and payment systems – all markets penetrated or dominated by retailers – suggest the scale of threat this poses to traditional financial institutions. This point is further underlined by the chapter's account of retailer inroads into financial services in the USA, Italy and Australia.

Chapter 6 by Dr Philip Dover develops the international perspective further by outlining the lessons to be learned from US experience in areas such as EFTPOS and debit cards, ATMs and Home and Office banking services. Whatever the European dimension created by the 1992 single market moves, many of the most important recent developments in financial services – credit cards, electronic banking, etc. – have originated in the USA. It seems likely that the USA will continue to be an important originator of ideas and trends. Consequently, Philip Dover's account of the failure of screen-based home banking in the USA, and his conclusions on the need for a broader home information service, are both timely and significant. But while his analysis underlines the barriers to consumer acceptance of radical technological innovations, it also makes clear the sometimes surprising strategic opportunities created by IT: the Japanese Nintendo electronic games company, for instance, and its plans to exploit its massive consumer base with additional home banking and shopping services.

Chapter 7 reinforces the points made in earlier chapters about the need for IT to be integrated into business strategy. It tackles the question of how such integration is to be achieved. In particular, it focuses on the connection, or lack of it, between the role of IT in formal strategic planning and its incorporation in the skills and products which actually create competitive advantage. Case studies of two companies – the Bank of Scotland and the Direct Line insurance company – highlight the way in which IT becomes an integral part of competitive strategy. Finally, the chapter examines the role of the IT function itself in the management of IT.

Chapter 2

The UK financial services marketplace

Harry Scarbrough

The central problem involved in managing IT is not the scale of investment it demands, nor even the problems of acquiring and controlling IT staff. It is the problem of relating IT use to corporate strategy. This has not always been a problem in financial services: in the 1950s and 1960s the strategies of the major firms were well defined, and, given steep rises in transaction volumes, the need for 'back office automation' was indisputable. The 1980s, however, saw far-reaching changes sweep through the sector. Deregulation and technological change had the simultaneous effect of increasing the level of strategic uncertainty, while expanding the range of technological options through which strategies could be pursued. This chapter addresses the strategies of the major players in the new market context and highlights their implications for the use of IT in products and delivery systems.

Up to the 1980s, the sector had been made up of a number of fairly well-defined industries – banking, building societies, insurance – each with its own distinctive products, institutional and professional structures and regulatory frameworks. There seemed to be a definable trajectory in each industry's development – banking, for instance, seemed to have entered the 'mature' phase of its life cycle, while building societies were still clearly in a growth phase.

One view of the 1980s changes is that they swept away all the pre-existing demarcations, and that all parts of the sector are now on a convergent and increasingly competitive path. Certainly, many of the old institutional and regulatory demarcations have been eliminated. However, the legacy of such demarcations remains strong in the segmenting of the marketplace, the design of products and the core skills of firms. Thus the argument for convergence needs to be set against the continuing influence of such factors on consumer perceptions, and on the strategies of financial service providers themselves.

In the long run, it seems, the strategies adopted by firms are likely to be a function of their current positions and their interaction with the changing competitive forces in the sector. In the remainder of this chapter we will outline how the key elements in this strategic equation relate to different parts of the sector. This will provide a basis for discussing the role of IT in the strategic development of the different players.

A SURVEY OF THE FINANCIAL SERVICES MARKETPLACE

Deregulation

The 1980s saw a plethora of regulatory changes: the Financial Services Act of 1986 and the Building Societies Act which came into force in 1987, together with 'Big Bang' in the City and the Social Security Act which gave an enormous stimulus to pensions business by increasing the portability of pensions.

One important consequence of this legislation for the marketing of insurance products was its incorporation of the principle of 'polarisation'. The latter created a requirement for companies to choose between operating as independent intermediaries – with a requirement to meet rigorous standards of 'know your client' and 'best advice' – or to opt to become 'tied' to the products of a particular company. This principle, innocuous enough in theory, was implemented in ways which seemed to disadvantage independent intermediaries. There was the prospect of one-sided commission disclosure, for instance, with brokers having to reveal their commission levels but their 'tied' competitors not under the same obligation.

Such legislative changes had a major impact on insurance companies. While the Social Security Act provided a tremendous stimulus to the marketing of personal pension products, the requirements of polarisation posed an important strategic challenge. There were strenuous efforts on the part of some life offices to maintain the role of independent intermediaries. Although some companies staked their survival on the continued efficacy of independent brokers, some of the larger firms hedged their bets and either set up their own sales forces or pursued strategic alliances with major outlets such as building societies.

Of the banks, only National Westminster of the Big Four plus Yorkshire Bank and the Royal Bank of Scotland decided to stay independent advisers. The other banks acquired SIB (Securities and Investment Board) agreement to allow 'conduit advice' – that is, they were allowed to market their own insurance products but also, where necessary, to pass on clients to independent broking subsidiaries.

In the building societies, policy decisions on polarisation were taken in the broader context of the product-market and institutional changes made possible by the 1980s legislation. Their attitude was more hesitant. At first, a number of major societies announced their intention of pursuing independent status, but subsequently many of them recanted and became tied outlets for the large insurance companies.

Another strategic issue confronting the building society industry in this period was the possibility of institutional change created by the Building Societies Act. Debate about the possible advantages of abandoning the 'mutual' form of ownership has been crystallised by the example set by one of the largest societies, the Abbey National. Having been one of the more aggressively expansive societies, the Abbey National chafed more than others under the remaining constraints – access to capital markets and so on – which mutual building society status imposed, and quickly obtained the consent of its members to convert to a public limited company and, in effect, to take on the status of a bank.

Even without institutional change, it became possible for building societies to offer a range of products which had hitherto been exclusive to the banks – of these the most important were current accounts and unsecured personal lending.

Overall, the effect of deregulation was to increase greatly the level of uncertainty within the sector. By increasing access to previously protected markets it created a threat of oversupply. This was all the greater as new entrants into a market segment would often focus on market share rather than profitability in the first instance. On the other hand, in certain contexts the new regulatory frameworks may have buttressed the position of the largest firms. It can be argued, for instance, that polarisation has favoured the largest insurance companies and banks, and that they have entrenched their dominant market position through various forms of strategic alliance.

Banking

A brief summary of the last 30 years in UK banking includes events such as the 1960s expansion of branch networks, the international diversification of the 1970s, and the market diversification of the 1960s and 1970s – the latter involving moves into credit cards, insurance, merchant banking and so on. All of these changes wrought their own effects within the banks. There were structural changes, for example, in the form of newly created international divisions and the addition of various subsidiaries. These product-market developments together with the balance-sheet advantages of separating out different business interests led to the emergence of multi-divisional retail banks within holding company structures as a standard pattern.

The pace of strategic change established in the 1970s was further accelerated in the 1980s, as the banks extended or initiated commitments on a number of fronts:

● The expansion of ATM networks.

- The large-scale redesign of branches, particularly the move to open-plan, customer-friendly premises.
- Further additions to product ranges and delivery systems.
- An even higher pitch of diversification; in 1982 Lloyds Bank became the first financial institution to buy an estate agency chain.
- Cost cutting in branch networks; attempts to eliminate staff and paperwork through cheque truncation and counter terminals. The automation of branch work – processing, administration and routine customer service.
- The development of branding for current accounts – Midland's Vector, Orchard and Meridian accounts, Lloyds' Classic account, and so on.

Credit cards

From their establishment in the UK in the late 1960s through Barclaycard, credit card businesses have become a major force in the financial sector. Credit cards revolutionise the information-gathering requirements of financial services. Where relationship banking allows creditworthiness to be assessed and adjusted with the information provided by a number of transactions, credit cards concentrate such an assessment into the initial decision to issue a card (Carter *et al.*, 1986). This together with the focus on a particular product permits the centralisation of information processing and a highly efficient infrastructure.

For the banks, credit cards provided an opportunity to build significant barriers to entry by adding economies of scope – their credit-scoring skills and customer information base – to economies of scale in information processing. Barclays in particular were able to exploit these barriers to entry, building on their innovatory introduction of Barclaycard in 1966 to establish a relatively dominant position. That dominance in turn prompted a competitive response from the other clearers, beginning with the launch of Access in 1972.

Competition was heightened by the regulatory changes of the 1980s and the more recent investigations by the Monopolies and Mergers Commission. This has helped to loosen the major banks' grip on the credit card business. In this context, those factors which encourage the diffusion of credit cards – the relative simplicity of the product and the tenuous relationship between provider and customer - may serve to increase the intensity of competition by permitting high levels of customer choice and mobility and the potential proliferation of credit card products. Increasing ease of access to credit card infrastructures through the opening up of the Visa and Mastercard networks, and the break-up of merchant acquiring monopolies, have encouraged proliferation, with many banks opting for 'duality' – that is, offering credit card users both Visa and Mastercard products. In the short run, at least, these moves reduced profitability. Barclaycard, for example, made £99 million profit in 1988, but in 1990 lost £4 million.

In this maturing product market, the squeeze on profit margins and the erosion of retailer-generated income have prompted the major banks to seek a redefinition of the credit card product. With consumers increasingly using their cards simply as a payment mechanism rather than as a source of credit – with the borrowing even on Barclaycard accounting for no more than 1 per cent of total private borrowing in the UK – the banks have responded first by promoting the use of debit cards (Connect and Switch) for payment purposes. Secondly, in what has been termed a 'knee jerk reaction' (*The Banker*, April 1991), they introduced small annual fees of £5 to £8, as a means both of generating much-needed income and of encouraging more lucrative credit-related card use. One immediate result, however, was a loss of customers. Lloyds Bank, which was in the vanguard of those introducing annual fees, found that it quickly lost 20 per cent of its cardholder base.

Insurance

The UK is Europe's second largest insurance market, and in volume, variety and sophistication of life and savings products it is pre-eminent. The industry is a major employer in the UK with around 285,000 employees.

The industry's product markets are broadly segmented between Life and General business, though a dozen or so 'composite' insurers of 10,000-plus employees do business in both areas.

Life and pensions business makes up around two-thirds of the sector in terms of income and is the most rapidly growing part of the industry. One of the major Life companies, Standard Life, controls interests accounting for around 2 per cent of the UK equity market. The marketing of Life business is divided up between the following:

- 'Industrial life' which is promoted and administered by a direct sales force – the Prudential, for example, has a sales force of around 12,000.
- 'High net worth' insurance of the kind marketed by Allied Dunbar and Abbey Life.
- The wide range of insurance products sold through the 100,000 or so intermediaries – accountants, lawyers, building societies – spread throughout the UK.

Although the industry contains a large number of firms, the bulk of the business is concentrated in the hands of a relatively small number, with just 20 firms accounting for 88 per cent of Life business, and the top 50 for over 98 per cent (Feeny and Knott, 1988).

While Life business was stimulated by 1980s deregulation and the marketing of a wider range of products – notably, personal pensions and unit-trust-related products – General business has been squeezed by the increasing scale of underwriting losses. The returns from investment management and the 'float' between premium receipt and claims settlement have become increasingly important. Ironically, the latter is gradually being reduced by the effect of IT on the speed and efficiency of claims processing.

The 1980s saw a number of insurance firms engaged in mergers and diversification. But despite the benefits arising out of some of these moves, the overall picture was dominated by what in retrospect appear to have been misguided strategic decisions. The Prudential company, for example, followed Lloyds Bank into the estate agency business only to be confronted by the late-1980s slump in the housing business. Eventually, the company was forced to sell off its estate agency chain at a loss of £334 million. General Accident's acquisition of a New Zealand insurance company met with equally costly failure: estimates suggest losses of around £200 million (*The Independent*, 18.4.91).

Building societies

The building societies benefited from both economic and regulatory changes in the 1980s. The boom in the housing market was a significant factor, and this was given added impact by legal factors such as the 1980 Housing Act encouraging the purchase of council houses, and the introduction of MIRAS (Mortgage Interest Relief At Source) in 1983 which encouraged a switch to endowment mortgages. The latter increased from about 20 per cent of the total in 1982 to 80 per cent in 1989. This gave a major impetus to the societies' commission earnings from the insurance companies.

The Building Societies Act came into force on 1 January 1987, allowing building societies, within limits, to own estate agencies and offer virtually all personal financial services, including unsecured loans and conveyancing. However, in the initial period many societies seemed to be wary of going too far beyond their traditional skills, and focused instead on reviewing their organisation and marketing in the light of the new regulatory and market environment.

CASE EXAMPLE:
LEEDS PERMANENT BUILDING SOCIETY

This mid-range society was just outside the group of the largest societies. It was neither focused on a specialist or local market, nor a full-range provider of services. It had, however, achieved significant growth in market share and profitability in the previous period.

In the late 1980s a number of key decisions were taken in response to the new market and regulatory environment facing the building society industry. First and foremost, a decision was taken to stay a mutual society and not to follow the Abbey National route and become a public limited company supervised by the Bank of

England. The Boston Consulting Group were brought in to advise on strategy, however, and the society examined a move into current accounts and transaction retail banking. This was rejected. Constraints included the 'horrendous' cost of launching current accounts — an estimated £50 per account — and the physical size of the average Leeds Permanent branch, which was only one-third the size of a typical Halifax or Abbey National branch.

But while the society decided to focus on its traditional core business, it was also adding to its product line incrementally. Significant costs, both of advertising and of business losses, were sustained by the society's move into credit card and estate agency business. At the same time, organisational restructuring was proceeding apace. A new structure was developed which removed a whole layer of management, while exploiting new management information systems. The branch network itself was pruned as 60 of the society's 481 branches were closed.

Source: *Financial Times*, January 1990.

One such building society was the Leeds Permanent, whose experience, described above, can be taken as fairly typical of the kinds of strategic decision which all societies had to confront in the late 1980s and early 1990s. Others, particularly in the smaller to medium-sized range, sought safety in numbers through mergers with like-minded peers. In doing so, they were perpetuating a long-term trend in the industry, as Table 2.1 outlines. The perceived advantages of mergers included the following:

- The benefits of national advertising.
- The ability to buy the latest technology.
- Membership of BACS and other money transmission groups.
- Cheap access to wholesale money markets.
- An improved ability to compete in post-1992 Europe (Wells, 1989).

But while societies pondered the new range of strategic options available to them, some saw the experience of the more adventurous societies as a timely

Table 2.1 Increasing concentration in the building society industry

Year	Number of societies
1900	2,286
1930	1,026
1960	726
1970	481
1980	273
1988	137

warning. For example, Nationwide Anglia's experience in developing a highly innovative current account – 'FlexAccount' – was not entirely positive. *The Independent* commented on Nationwide's experience:

> As for FlexAccount, the society must wish it had been a little less flexible in the way it introduced this service . . . it is always difficult to feed in a new service such as this through a control system which has not been accustomed to coping with such a service. It is unkind to say that the society was so eager to exploit its clever marketing idea that it lost sight of sound banking practice, but the scale of loss is such that it is hard to reach any other conclusion. (12.6.90)

COMPETITIVE FORCES

One of the principal causes of sectoral uncertainty is the shifting pattern of competitive forces. In broad terms we can see that, as product markets open up and evolve, the competitive rules of the game are likely to be shaped by:

- The economics of cross-segment delivery channels.
- Customer inertia.
- Barriers to entry (technology, skills, marketing) for different segments.

However, within this economic framework, the dynamics of competition in financial services remain highly complex. There are oligopolistic factors, which mean that the rules of competition are often established by the strategies of the major players. Also, the emergence of this loosely integrated sector has created a dynamic of its own. Added to this is the importance of infrastructural factors within the sector. The banks' dominance of payment mechanisms once gave them a built-in advantage in attracting deposits. Now this has been eroded by the opening up of the clearing house structure to non-bank players.

Although deregulation has not entirely eliminated the demarcations between the different industrial groupings, it has increased the level of product overlap and direct competition. The rivalry between banks and building societies, in particular, has progressively increased throughout the 1970s and 1980s.

This increasing rivalry was reflected initially in a series of strategic moves made by one industry group against the other. Thus in 1980 the banks used their newly acquired freedom from corset restrictions on lending to attack the huge home loans/mortgage market – a market which accounts for the bulk of personal lending in the UK.

This initiative, however, was countered by strategic thrusts from other industry groups. In the early 1980s high-interest bank accounts were offered by unit trusts in conjunction with merchant banks, and a number of building societies offered high-interest savings accounts combined with a cheque book.

The attack on the banks' current account base has been intensified by some of the largest building societies moving into this market in the wake of the

Building Society Act. Although all but the biggest societies have been deterred by the cost of operating current accounts, the entry of organisations such as Nationwide Anglia, Abbey National and, most recently, the Halifax is likely to create a significant competitive force. Within a year or so of launching a current account, Nationwide's FlexAccount had racked up 1 million account-holders, while Abbey National had achieved 800,000 for its product.

The impact of these various moves has been greatly to increase direct competition both in the provision of services and in cost terms. The extension of opening hours by the major banks, for instance, has been matched by the extension of services in the building societies: the deployment of ATMs and the provision of direct debits and standing orders. At the same time the pressure on margins and costs has greatly intensified. Interest rates on savings accounts have become more competitive and current accounts have become more attractive than ever before. The development of 'free in credit' banking in the mid-1980s was quickly followed by the provision of interest on current accounts – a move initiated by Nationwide Anglia and imitated for defensive reasons by the large clearing banks.

A more comforting prospect for the banks is that in at least one area – unsecured personal lending – they are likely to retain a commanding position for some time to come. This reflects both their long-established skills in this area and the relative inexperience of building societies – inexperience which is likely to prove costly in the early stages of development.

Costs

The entry of building societies into banking services has had a clear effect on competitive cost norms within the sector. Even though the lower cost base of the building societies was attributable in part to their more specialised operations, it none the less provides an important strategic benchmark for the banks.

Meanwhile, the application of IT offers the potential both for reducing branch costs and for reducing the need for branches themselves through the development of non-branch delivery systems. Banks and building societies alike are being forced to review the historical legacy of branch networks which were developed in a less competitive era. Programmes of limited reductions in branch numbers have become a standard feature of the major banks. At the same time, and as we discuss in Chapter 3, there has been a restructuring of operations such that, in banks such as Barclays and Midland, back-office work in the branches has been concentrated in a small number of processing centres.

But as banks seek to develop new electronic delivery systems, yet protect their conventional branch infrastructures, they run the risk not only of spiralling costs but also of technological leapfrogging by new entrants into the sector (Howcroft and Lavis, 1987).

Diversification

It is easy to overstate the importance of diversification as a conscious strategy. Diversification, as was noted earlier, has been happening for a long time in banking and to a lesser extent in other areas too. Often diversification moves are defensive or opportunistic reactions to changes in the marketplace rather than part of a long-run strategy. Defined simply as moves away from an existing product-market portfolio, diversification can occur both through the organic means of product development and through corporate acquisition. The motives behind diversification are equally diverse and range from the pragmatic to the strategic:

- Add-ons to existing product ranges: for example, over-the-counter loans, house contents insurance, etc.
- Convenience: to enhance the attractiveness of the existing product range.
- Complementarity: a logical extension of the existing range such as traveller's cheques.
- New product markets: a relatively quick means of entering new product areas.
- Synergy: the exploitation of informational or marketing overlap in the production or marketing of product-ranges.

Defensiveness in the face of strategic uncertainty has been the keynote to many recent diversification moves. For example, the frantic acquisition of estate agency chains by the larger banks, building societies and insurance companies might have been prompted for some by a strategic awareness of the agencies' potential for cross-selling mortgage business. For many others, however, it seems to have been a short-term and defensive reaction to their competitors' behaviour: in short, the 'follow my lemming' syndrome.

Even where diversification was aimed at producing a well-balanced portfolio of businesses, there was often little attempt to exploit the synergistic opportunities of cross-selling that this created. Until recently, for instance, many banks took a department store approach to their corporate portfolios. Their diverse activities were seen as separate concerns with little attempt to present or manage them as an integrated range of services.

There are powerful operational reasons for such an approach. Although an insurance company such as Abbey Life gains advantages of reputation and capital resource from being part of the Lloyds retail bank group, as long as bank branches are geared to banking and transaction services it may be difficult for any insurance company to exploit cross-marketing opportunities to the full.

At a higher level, however, there are signs that a diversified business portfolio may create an important informational synergy between its component parts. Barclays, for example, have developed a 'Customer Information System' which places all customer relationships with the bank on to one database. This allows the direct mail targeting of products based on individual circumstances. Significantly, customers are being invited to opt out of rather than opt into the system.

This kind of move, which is dependent upon the database technology discussed in Chapter 4, suggests that informational advantages may be added to the usual risk-spreading and financial economies associated with diversified portfolios.

Alliances

Apart from outright mergers and acquisitions – notable recent examples of which are Britannia building society's acquisition of the mutual FS Assurance life office, or the creation of the Lloyds Abbey Life financial conglomerate – a distinctive feature of the recent period has been the emergence of inter-industry alliances of the kind outlined in Table 2.2.

These alliances do not seem to be a means of re-establishing the cartel arrangements that used to prevail in individual industries. In most cases they seem to be responses to increasing uncertainty within the sector rather than attempts to establish market control. They also reflect the new patterns of collaborative infrastructure and distribution which are emerging in the sector as deregulation and product innovation create new marketing opportunities or threats. Thus, we find the polarisation principle encouraging alliances between insurance firms and building societies, in which the latter become major marketing channels for the former.

The formation of strategic alliances reflects change and restructuring within the sector. Not only does it allow organisations to supplement the geographical spread of their business – an important factor behind the links between Scottish banks and English building societies in the early 1980s – but it also produces marketing economies of scale in the process. Moreover, such joint ventures may provide the kind of admixture of technological and business expertise needed for important product innovations. The link between Merrill Lynch and BankOne of the USA in the development of the 'cash management account' is an important case in point.

Table 2.2 Strategic alliances in financial services

Halifax Building Society – Standard Life insurance
Woolwich Building Society – Sun Alliance insurance
Alliance and Leicester – Scottish Amicable insurance
Midland Bank – Commercial Union insurance

Harry Scarbrough

CONCLUSIONS

The changes of the 1980s have stimulated a great deal of strategic activity in financial services. Positions of strength have been turned into positions of weakness. The banks' control of the clearing system, for example, which previously created a barrier to entry, is now seen as inhibiting their ability to achieve distinctive market identity and differentiation (Howcroft and Lavis, 1986). The opening up of the clearing system may allow more marketing-oriented firms to achieve high market profiles. Similarly, the elimination of institutional constraints on the provision of retail financial services may make it possible for new IT-based entrants into the market to leapfrog the costly and sometimes outdated delivery systems of the major branch networks.

Clearly, in this context banks and building societies are forced to be proactive. Banks can no longer be passive deposit-takers but must become active providers of financial services. This may lead to the more realistic pricing of services. No longer can payment services, for instance, be subsidised by the interest garnered from 'free' current account deposits: up to the late 1980s, this covered 60–65 per cent of the costs of offering current accounts (Howcroft and Lavis, 1987).

These changes, together with the pressures of cost competition and differentiation described earlier, threaten a fundamental restructuring of financial services. Markets may be segmented between those products which depend on personal relationships, and those which can be standardised as self-service or 'off-the-shelf' commodities. Competitive pressures and technological change may make it difficult to sustain those products which do not fit the organisation's particular competence, be it efficiency or special skills (see Figure 2.1). Certainly, IT has the potential to support either approach. In later

	COMMODITY SERVICES	PERSONAL SERVICES
EFFICIENCY	Processing systems Self-service products, e.g. ATMs	
SPECIAL COMPETENCE		Customer information systems Expert systems

Source: Pollock (1985).

Figure 2.1 A strategy matrix for financial services

chapters, for instance, we describe the use of information and expert systems to enhance 'relationship banking'. Alternatively, customer-friendly product development and delivery systems may be applied to the provision of commodity and self-service products.

However, unless the potential of IT is geared to a clear-headed competitive strategy, it is unlikely to be effective. What makes this even more critical is that our prognosis for the sector as a whole has highlighted important changes in sectoral boundaries. While entry barriers were being lowered in the 1980s, exit barriers were being raised by the kinds of technological investment needed to offer payment systems and other products. Given this kind of structural change, the intensity of competition in the sector seems likely to increase, and with it the need to deploy IT effectively, efficiently and imaginatively.

Chapter 3

IT, products and infrastructures in financial services

Harry Scarbrough

There is no doubt that IT applications are crucial to the development of the financial services sector. However, the significance of IT does not derive from the intrinsic merits of the technology alone. After all, financial institutions are selling services not technology. In that context, IT is important only in so far as it supports business objectives and operations.

It follows that the actual and potential application of IT in financial services is as much to do with the nature of the sector and of financial products in general, as it is to do with the technology itself. It is out of the *interaction* between such sectoral features and the characteristics of the technology that enduring and competitive applications emerge.

In reviewing the application of IT to products, delivery systems and infrastructures, we will begin with a review of the sector as a whole, and those features of the sector which exert a strong influence upon patterns of IT use.

This review must start from an analysis of the underlying structural features of financial services. Although, as we noted earlier, there remain important distinctions between the approach and product range of different types of financial services organisation, such distinctions will no longer be supported by high regulatory barriers, but will be tested in the marketplace. Within that marketplace, the structural features of customer needs for financial products and the economics of meeting those needs are likely to become key parameters of both internal segments and external boundaries.

SECTORAL FEATURES AND IT APPLICATIONS

The age of some of the largest financial institutions is a pointer to the deep historical roots of the sector. Many of the key features of financial services, including major product 'innovations' such as the current account, can be traced back to the seventeenth and eighteenth centuries. It was in this period that the development of banking institutions permitted the abstraction of money from particular physical commodities such as gold, or from promissory relationships between particular individuals. The banks helped to create social acceptability for the abstract relationships embodied in 'deposit money' and 'negotiable bearer certificates'.

Although the social acceptability of financial instruments is now taken for granted, it is worth noting this historical basis of trust and relationships. All savings products, for example, be they high interest chequing accounts or endowment policies, depend ultimately upon the customer's belief in the trustworthiness of the institution to which his or her savings are committed. This element of trust has long been enshrined in the cultural and occupational make-up of financial institutions, where prudence and a sense of custodianship have been seen as important virtues. Where that trust is violated, however – as we saw, for instance, in the BCCI affair – the foundations of financial institutions are undermined.

In addition to the cultural dimension of financial services, there is also an important political dimension. The importance of financial institutions to the operation of the monetary economy, and hence to all economic activity, creates a political role which is reflected in close regulation by the state. The most visible expression of this is the link between the government's setting of interest rate levels, and the activity and profitability of lending institutions. Ironically, the 1980s period of deregulation served only to underline the impact of government policy on the sector (Moran, 1991).

We can define the services offered by the sector as essentially threefold:

- Payment services.
- Wealth accumulation.
- Security.

Because such services are focused on the manipulation of money – a 'universal commodity' or generic instrument for satisfying human wants – they take a distinctive form. This is expressed in some of the key structural features of the sector, which we shall now consider.

Non-specific material basis

Once money became an abstract commodity, products and services based around it were similarly freed from material constraints. Relationships or, more specifically, *information* about relationships is thus the lifeblood of the sector. The only material constraints arising out of the need to process such information are those defined by the most up-to-date technology. Products can be readily collapsed into each other, and wide ranges of products offered from a single branch. The average bank branch may offer up to 300 different

products, constrained only by the information-processing capacity of technology or, more likely, the capacity of branch staff themselves.

The malleability of financial services has tremendous implications for the
application of IT. It means, for instance, that the ability to develop and modify
information-processing systems becomes one of the critical constraints on
business development.

Information-based services

The variety and intensity of the information flows involved in financial services
create major opportunities for the application of IT in both product design and
distribution. The use of IT, however, is subject to the paradox that, although IT
applications may be becoming increasingly pervasive, they rarely represent
major innovations in service content. More often than not the use of IT
involves the automation, repackaging or more effective delivery of the same
basic financial services. This is reflected in the development of both ATMs and
electronic banking.

Intermediary functions

Financial institutions operate as intermediaries between lenders and borrowers. Both historically and in profit terms, the provision of services is secondary
to this intermediary function. Payment systems and other financial products
were developed out of the need to attract depositors and lenders so that the
intermediary function could be performed.

This go-between role emphasises the importance of maintaining *relationships*
with lenders and borrowers – a process which is still reflected in the local
community role played by bank and building society managers.

Infrastructures

Like all services, financial services require some form of distribution infrastructure. The character of that infrastructure is determined by the variety and
quality of the information flows it is required to support. The extensive
two-way flows of information involved in many banking products, for
example, require localised branch networks and face-to-face contact. They can
be contrasted with the much more truncated flows of information involved in
credit card businesses. This helps to explain the centralised, 'factory'-style use
of IT which is found in credit card operations.

The implications of these structural features are summarised in Table 3.1.

Table 3.1 Structural features of financial services and the use of IT

Structural features of financial services sector	Implications for market structure	Implications for IT use
Non-specific material basis for service	Products readily collapsible, not easily differentiated	IT all-pervasive
Service functions	Branch networks, importance of customer relationships	Long-term, infrastructural investments
Intermediary functions	Product development and costing functions intertwined	Centre–periphery structure for delivery systems
Sophisticated planning and payment systems	Clearing systems depend on co-operation for economies of scale	Costing of IT based on strategic criteria

SECTORAL FEATURES AND COMPETITION

Porter (1980) argues that competitive advantage is gained through one of three generic strategies: cost leadership, differentiation or segmentation (that is, applying cost leadership or differentiation to a particular segment). Although IT is often used to support these aims, the patterns of IT use in financial services suggest that the competitive application of technology may be more complex than such nostrums allow. This seems to be because competitive forces are mediated by the underlying structural features of the sector. Important tensions and constraints arise from these features, as we outline below.

Service–intermediary tensions

The financial importance of the intermediary function means that retail products and services do not always cover their costs. In banking, many products do not cover their costs, but are marketed in order to maintain the kind of customer relationships on which income-earning activities depend. Similarly, in general insurance profits have come increasingly from investment income, while underwriting has become a consistently loss-making function.

Although the customer has benefited from the provision of many services effectively free of charge at the point of use, there are potential conflicts between the *service* and the *intermediary* dimensions of the sector. These are being aggravated by the increasing levels of competition. For example, while competition has led to the provision of current accounts offering interest, it has also eroded the 'float' available to banks (the interest derived from previously 'free' deposits). This has reduced the income derived from such accounts and has encouraged moves towards lucrative fee-based services and the pricing of services. The latter is made more difficult, however, because the first-mover in such situations inevitably attracts competitive disadvantages.

Co-operation and competition

The economics of payment mechanisms and the requirements of a clearing system create a need for co-operation between organisations. In the past, this need, combined with the oligopolistic structure of the banking industry, acted to constrain inter-organisational competition. The sector was characterised by uniformity in pricing and 'co-operative behaviour defensive strategies' (Howcroft and Lavis, 1987). The latter were reflected in the tendency for the major banks to move together in their strategic forays. There were concerted moves into house mortgage and 'high net worth' segments, for instance, and the formation of alliances with co-operative groups such as Visa and Mastercard.

Even in a deregulated context, where cartel arrangements have been eliminated, co-operation continues to have its attractions. There are significant economies to be gained from creating co-operatively based services which greatly enhance customer benefits while spreading the costs between a large number of participants. For example, it is significant that ATMs, which were once seen as an instrument of competition, are now a largely non-competitive commodity within the sector. Three major networks – Matrix, Link and 4-ATM – have emerged, increasing the benefit to the customer, but largely eliminating any direct competitive advantage.

The ATM example suggests that, when IT is used to support commodity products, it creates at best a kind of negative competitive power. No direct competitive advantage flows from such applications, but barriers to entry are raised and those who do not deploy such systems are penalised.

But the factors encouraging such co-operative investments in IT are increasingly being outweighed by the perceived imperatives of competition. Attempts to proceed without allies and achieve competitive advantage through product innovation may undermine the co-operative effort on which large, costly and standardised infrastructures are built.

The classic example of this problem can be seen in the rise and fall of EFTPOS UK, which was overtaken by the banks' own competitive developments. When EFTPOS finally collapsed there were 350 EFTPOS terminals in the UK as against 80,000 of the banks' own terminals. The problem is apparent also in the attempts to establish comprehensive on-line quotation systems for insurance brokers in the early 1980s. Various individualistic attempts by major insurance companies failed because they could not deliver the standardisation and comparability which such systems require. Industry-standard systems emerged only with the entry of third-party network providers. The latter were able to create a profitable niche out of the insurance companies' inability to co-operate.

Product differentiation and customer relationships

The importance of relationships and the non-material basis of financial services place constraints on the marketing of financial products. Although competition in the current account area, for instance, has led to significant forms of market segmentation – services being aimed at segments such as young people, 'high net worth' individuals and so on – attempts at competitive differentiation through product 'branding' have had a limited effectiveness. As yet, it remains unclear whether the *branding* of current account products – for example, Midland's Vector, Meridian and Orchard accounts, and Lloyds' Classic and Gold Service – represents anything more than the *labelling* of the product.

Even product innovation may have limited potential for competitive differentiation. Service innovations are not patentable and can often be easily copied – within, say, six months of the product being launched in banking, and a year or so in insurance. Low barriers to entry coupled with the ease of product imitation in some personal financial markets have led to a concern with secrecy and speed in new product development. In life insurance, for instance, the most common approach to new product development is to copy competitors' products. The test marketing of new products is consequently rare because of fears of competitor reaction (Watkins, 1988).

Bundling of products, systems, infrastructures

Competitiveness is often understood in terms of the cost or differentiation achieved by individual, discrete products. But in financial services such a focus may be misleading. First, the products themselves are made up of a variety of services: for example, the credit card is both a payment instrument and a means of obtaining credit. Secondly, there are a number of incentives for financial service firms to offer a range of products through a particular delivery system. These incentives include the information spillovers and customer convenience resulting from personal contact. Some of the products, indeed, may have as much to do with developing a relationship with the customer as with profitability *per se*. Loss-leader accounts aimed specifically at young people are one such product.

From the service provider's point of view, there are economies of scope to be achieved from such an approach, as well as the more efficient utilisation of a particular system. Delivery systems themselves may be grouped around an underlying infrastructure, such that the branch network, for instance, becomes the underpinning for a range of technological and human delivery systems.

There are, of course, countervailing factors which promote the unbundling of services – notably, the trend towards multiple account holding by customers, and the technological and economic advantages of disaggregating products, systems and infrastructures (Steiner and Teixeira, 1990). However, these are limited by the ability of existing infrastructures to 'lock in' customers. One example would be the procedures associated with changing direct debits and standing orders.

The dependence on infrastructures and the constraints on product differentiation have encouraged strategic development around the control of delivery systems and infrastructures. Although a variety of products have been developed to exploit the relationships thus created, the marketing of products outside that privileged relationship has not been high on the strategic agenda.

These strategic tendencies have had important implications for both the structure and the technology of financial service organisations. At the structural level, the predominant managerial roles have gone to occupations with skills in financial intermediation – bankers, actuaries and so on – and other functional areas such as marketing have been comparatively neglected. Moreover, organisation structures have been based around the functional tasks needed to support the financial intermediation and delivery infrastructures at the centre of strategic activity. Product-based arrangements such as product divisions have consequently never been a feature of the major bank or building society structures.

IT AND INFRASTRUCTURES

The most important consequence of these factors for the use of IT is to do with the importance of infrastructures. This has two important effects on the pattern of IT use. The first is that the shape of IT systems reflects the demands of branch networks, the standard configuration being that of a corporate IT function supporting a central mainframe plus distributed branch systems. Relatedly, a good deal of IT spending is aimed at supporting branch networks. As described in Chapter 7, computing power was originally applied to the automation of back-office and clerical work in the branches. In the current period, it has also spread into front-office applications such as branch information systems which shape the customer interface. One result of the increasing spread of IT into branches is steadily increasing IT budgets – a total of £136 million at Abbey National alone in 1990.

A second consequence of the use of IT to support infrastructures, however, is that, with the honourable exception of front-office applications, a good deal of the expenditure involved has no direct competitive effect. The payment systems and transaction processing which such infrastructures incorporate demand high levels of spending just to maintain efficiency and keep pace with increasing volumes. Consequently, a good deal of IT spending is concentrated on the kind of transaction-oriented back-office work which still characterises branch operations. In the late 1980s it was estimated that 60 per cent of bank staff and 60 per cent of bank costs of the London clearing banks was committed to back-office functions (Howcroft and Lavis, 1987).

Moreover, as we noted of ATMs earlier, payment-based products promote co-operation rather than competition, and as a result become non-competitive staples within the product range. Their competitive effect is simply to raise barriers to entry. Even in the USA, as Steiner and Teixeira (1990) note, 65 per cent of systems expense supports funds movement, while only 10 per cent goes into potentially competitive functions: 'The vast bulk of systems investments support products or services that are commodities throughout the industry' (p. 45).

Branch networks: banks and building societies

Branch networks play an important role in financial services. Even in a period which has seen tremendous growth in the development of centralised financial services such as credit cards, personal loans and vehicle finance, branch networks continue to be a highly effective means of reaching the customer:

- Instilling customer confidence.
- Providing economies of scope and cross-selling opportunities.
- Retaining increasingly mobile customers.
- Providing an accessible and flexible customer interface.

Indeed, branch networks are a major barrier to entry, and cause of oligopoly, in certain financial markets. Citibank of the USA, for instance, has attempted to enter the UK banking market three times in the last 20 years. Each time the dominance of the major banks' networks has been a major barrier.

As indicated in Table 3.2 below, the main High Street banks currently have 11,927 branches. Their current operations are a product of evolution over the last 20 to 30 years. Branches were originally developed partly to act as a customer interface and partly as the deposit-gathering stage in the intermediation function.

Branches developed as relatively independent institutions, each one in effect a mini-bank offering a whole range of services on a local basis. As little as 20 years ago, cashing a cheque in another branch of the same bank required a special arrangement. When automation was extended to the branches in the 1960s and 1970s these characteristics led to the development of systems based on the overnight batch processing of account-based information (Hendry, 1987). Significantly, this historical background helped to produce important competitive constraints on the current operations of branches (see Table 3.3).

Table 3.2 Bank and building society branches and cash machines (end 1989)

	No. of branches	No. of cash machines
Abbey National	690	858
Bank of Scotland	527	330
Barclays Bank	2,645	2,193
Lloyds Bank	2,184	2,184
Midland Bank	2,042	1,868
National Westminster	2,997	2,583
Royal Bank of Scotland	842	646
All building societies	6,236	2,918

Source: Banking Information Service.

Table 3.3 Constraints on competitiveness of bank branches

- Transaction- and procedure-oriented branch operations.
- Constraints on the kind of on-line, real-time information processing which is becoming a feature of some of the most advanced products.
- Central information storage based on accounts rather than customers.
- Branches as bureaucratic and unfriendly interfaces rather than attractive retail space.
- A tradition of generalist rather than segmented branch provision.

In contrast, building society branches have fewer operational constraints. After a rapid increase – 10 per cent p.a. – in branch numbers in the 1970s, the rate of opening plateaued in the 1980s. Building society branches enjoy important advantages over the banks, particularly in their standardisation of processes and specialisation. This allowed LANs (Local Area Networks) and office systems to be extensively deployed, increasing branch efficiency.

Paradoxically, it was the earlier regulatory constraints on building societies which encouraged their early adoption of sophisticated on-line systems linked to central computers. The building societies, in common with the TSB, operated passbook accounts. Customers were not allowed to go into the red, and consequently their passbooks had to be updated from the computer each time a transaction was made. The on-line counter terminals involved in this data capture allowed the multi-branching of customers.

In both banks and building societies, the branch networks are at the forefront of current competitive developments, as follows.

Cost reduction

Increasing competition has inevitably encouraged cost-cutting in banking, and all the major banks are committed to programmes aimed at reducing the ratio of costs to income. This involves the pruning of branch networks and the reform of management structures. Most important, it encompasses a profound change in emphasis away from payments-processing and back-office work towards the more proactive marketing of services. Midland Bank has installed machines capable of clearing 60,000 cheques an hour in 13 centres to remove a layer of work from branch back offices. There is an acute awareness among the banks of the need for a shift towards a more lucrative, market-oriented use of their human and property resources, and this is reflected in, for example, reductions in staff numbers, the centralisation of back-office work and the redeployment of branch staff into marketing roles.

Customer interface

Both banks and building societies have paid a good deal of attention to branch design. This is aimed at making them more customer-friendly – more open-plan, less bandit-screened. In addition, banks have sought to exploit to the full the opportunities for cross-selling and personal contact which branches create. In many cases, this has involved both the widening of the product range and the reorganisation of work within the branch. The latter generally has two main components: first, the increased use of automation and the provision of branch information systems to allow counter staff to focus on customer service rather than transactional procedures; and secondly, the creation of specialist customer service roles aimed at marketing the new range of products.

These changes involve considerable shifts in skills and work organisation. They place particular demands on the use of technology given the transaction-oriented nature of the previous generations of banking systems. At branch level, such demands are satisfied by the provision of new information systems based on the customer and not the account. One of the largest such programmes is National Westminster's installation of around 21,000 VDUs in its branches. The advantages of such systems are generally seen as:

- Reducing costs.
- Improving service quality.
- Providing a marketing edge.
- Coping with volume growth and product introductions.

Previously information on customers might be stored in any of 12 different places within a branch: address book, lending register, accounts index, borrowing record and so on. Just answering a simple question about a customer's account might take 15 minutes to gather up all the details.

Implementing such systems, however, involves significant changes at the centre too, as organisations develop customer databases to drive the new information system. Databases greatly strengthen corporate management's understanding of its customer base and its ability to target particular groups through non-branch methods.

But in the process of developing such systems, there may be important organisational implications, particularly in the relationship between branches and central management. As IT allows information to flow both ways, there is no technological imperative to such organisational changes. The new technology may actually allow certain head office functions to be delegated to branches. For example, the introduction of expert systems for fire risk evaluation and rate setting allows decisions to be devolved from insurance head offices to branches. At the Sun Alliance company over 600 underwriters use an expert system for advice on assessing commercial risks. In banking too, such systems are a valuable management tool. The Midland Bank uses an IBM mainframe-based Credit Assessment System. This assesses loans, handles renewals semi-automatically and calculates repayment levels and schedules.

Conversely, by providing corporate management with information on branch profitability and management performance, IT may lead to tighter control of branches by decreasing branch manager autonomy in the granting of loans and in customer relations.

Segmentation and restructuring

The organisational clout of the branch and of branch management is also threatened by new forms of market segmentation. Some services needing less frequent or less local contact may be centralised or regionalised; hence the growth in central banking services and the moves towards 'hub-satellite' branch banking at Lloyds, Barclays and Midland. The latter move is aiming to differentiate between the mass, retail market and more specialised customers, especially small and medium-sized businesses.

The reorganisation of branch networks is being accompanied by restructuring within management. There have been major changes both within branches and at regional level. At Midland Bank, for instance, the number of regional directors has been cut by 50 per cent, while the TSB sacked 103 regional directors in 1989 alone.

The overall thrust of these changes, apart from countering the lower cost base of the building societies, seems to be aimed at shifting the role of branch networks from being relatively passive deposit-takers and payments processors to being much more aggressive marketing outlets for financial services.

Although branch networks remain pre-eminent for a wide range of financial products, it is equally important to recognise that technology and other factors are starting to erode some of their traditional advantages. The role played by branches in terms of customer communications and product delivery is steadily being usurped by new methods and media. In banks and building societies, this is illustrated by the ability of ATMs to provide an increasing range of services literally outside the branch itself.

INFRASTRUCTURES IN INSURANCE

Given the nature of the product, the infrastructural needs of insurance firms are different from those of banks. Large-scale, infrastructural investments in IT are not such a significant feature of the insurance industry: Feeny and Knott (1988), for instance, estimate the IT budgets of some of the larger insurance firms at around the £50 million mark compared to the billions needed by the major banks. Even so, IT is a major element of expenditure for the insurance industry: around 2 per cent of gross premium income or 10–15 per cent of administration expenses.

The recent period has created significant new demands for the use of IT in insurance. On one hand, regulatory changes and rapid growth in both the volume and variety of insurance products has created important implications for central processing and information storage. In order to improve the quality of customer service, insurance companies have also followed the customer database route, rewriting and adapting their software from a policy to a customer basis. Other new IT applications have also been parameter-based, conferring the following advantages:

- Reducing the time between the introduction of a new product and the development of administrative support.
- Supporting a wider range of more flexible products.
- Providing more detailed information about customer lifestyle and status.

At the same time, IT has increasingly been used to underpin the marketing of insurance products, either through support for direct sales forces or through networks linking insurance firms and intermediaries.

An example of the use of IT in direct sales comes from Allied Dunbar, which began by installing PCs in its sales offices programmed with some simple, illustrative examples of pensions and life policies. This unexpectedly created an interest from customers who wanted to explore different financial options on a 'what if' basis. Now personal computers programmed with options and examples are becoming part of the essential tools of the job for insurance salespeople.

In the intermediaries area, some of the most notable innovations came from Friends Provident, which developed the Gladis system in the 1970s to provide policy quotations and facilitate policy issue at branch level. Gladis was said to have increased the Friends Provident market share from 1.9 to 4.2 per cent in six years. In the 1980s Gladis was further expanded to become the Frentel system. This used viewdata to extend the company's services into the offices of agents. Frentel provides an on-line quotation service, query facilities, messaging and sales documentation to both branch offices and brokers.

A further boost to the use of IT by intermediaries came with the liberalisation of the UK telecoms market in the early 1980s. After an initial wave of attempts by some of the larger firms to develop their own intermediary systems, the intermediaries' needs for standardisation and comprehensiveness encouraged the development of third-party networks. In 1985, 16 companies joined PINS (Prestel Insurance Network and Service), which used British Telecom's Prestel network to distribute on-line quotations to intermediaries. Some brokers were linked directly to mainframe computers.

Another important move came with the development of Istel's Inview. This used viewdata technology and, although less technically sophisticated than some of the large firms' offerings, it furnished the bigger intermediaries, especially the building societies, with the kind of comprehensive, easy-to-use system that they had been looking for.

HOME AND OFFICE SERVICES

Twenty of the UK's 630 banks and building societies offer home and office services, and there are nearly 1 million customers in the UK. The relative success of different product offerings is highly variable. For instance, National Westminster's Action Line has 31,000 users, while TSB Speedlink has 250,000 users.

In technical terms, there has been an important progression in the way in which such services are delivered. After the early 1980s launch by the Bank of Scotland and the Nottingham Building Society of a home banking system based on the Prestel public viewdata system, subsequent developments polarised into two main camps.

On the one hand, there were telephone-based automated services using either tone-pad plus a voice response, or more sophisticated voice recognition techniques to connect customers to a computer. The latest addition to such services is Midland Bank's First Direct service, which has picked up around 100,000 customers. However, this product has moved away from automation by using human operators to interface with customers, providing services such as bill payment, loans and foreign exchange. On the other hand, screen-based services tended to shift away from the public viewdata route either to British Telecom's VANS (Value Added Network Systems) or to a direct linkage with the bank's central computers.

The strategic implications of home and office services are still uncertain, but they are potentially explosive for the sector – something which is reflected in the already large amounts invested in developing the current highly diverse array of home and office services. The Midland Bank, for instance, spent £6 million on promotion alone in the first three months after the launch of First Direct.

Given the financial investments and long-term thinking involved, home and office services pose the strategic challenge of IT in its most acute form. As such, they provide a useful object of study for assessing the different ways in which the strategic implications of an IT-based product can be assessed. Four different perspectives on the strategy–technology connection are outlined below:

- *Technological leadership*: what are the advantages of being first down the learning curve, or indeed of just following on behind?
- *Technological choice*: a range of technological permutations are available for home and office services – what are the implications of a commitment to a particular route?
- *Technology diffusion*: what factors influence the consumer's adoption of this new product?
- *Product–process life cycle*: how are these new banking products and their associated delivery systems likely to evolve over time?

Technological leadership

In terms of product innovation, financial service firms are heavily reliant on a range of technology suppliers whose products are available to all. Also, the product innovations generated by financial institutions are not patentable, and are therefore highly vulnerable to imitation.

Given these factors, a company's ability to create and sustain a genuine technological lead seems limited. Far more important are the relative advantages of being the 'first mover' in a new area. In essence, many of these come down to the company's positioning in the process of learning and adjustment that precedes the establishment of clear competitive rules and definable market segments. In the instance of home and office services, the pioneers learned important lessons about marketing such a product – what type of customer would be interested, their needs, and the importance of emphasising the service rather than the technology in advertising.

But it is equally important to recognise that in this context being a follower rather than a leader has its attractions too. The followers in this case were also able to derive useful lessons, not only from their own limited experiments but also from the pioneers' experience. They learned of the potential security problems of using viewdata systems, the potential size and composition of the market and so on. More generally, followers also benefit from awareness of the leaders' mistakes, the availability of tried and tested technology, and even the ability to leapfrog the technology to which the leaders become committed.

Technological choice

As Figure 3.1 indicates, home and office services involve the assembly of infrastructure, delivery system and final product. This means that there are a large number of technical permutations from which firms can choose. There are two crucial aspects to the exercise of technological choice in this context.

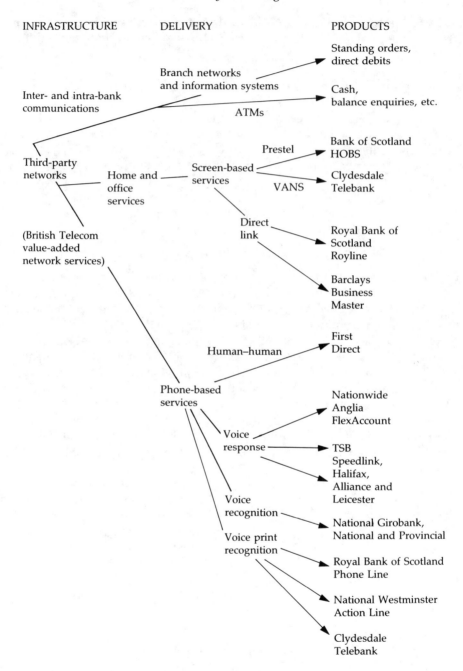

Figure 3.1 Electronic banking: technology choice

The first is to do with the hierarchical relationship between infrastructure, delivery system and product. A choice of infrastructure imposes constraints on the potential delivery system, which in turn influences the range of possible products which can be developed. Thus, to take a couple of examples, the use of a public viewdata system may create constraints on the level of security obtainable for a particular product. Similarly, the use of, say, leased lines to deliver a screen-based product involves the user having access to a PC and a modem – which is a limitation on the potential market for such a product.

Although the versatility of telecommunications infrastructures may impose fewer specific, technical constraints on products than do delivery systems, even here there may be economic and institutional constraints arising from, for example, the use of a third-party network. The latter may have an influence on the costs and quality of service which are outside the service provider's control.

The second impact of technology choice is more to do with sunk costs and the way in which a firm's commitment to a particular technological route creates investments in skills and technologies which can be changed only with the greatest difficulty. Branch networks themselves are perhaps the classic instance of this form of technology choice, but much the same thing applies to home and office services where the set-up and promotional costs of a particular product create a need to recoup that investment over time.

This kind of consideration, of course, may come into conflict with some of the above-noted implications of technology choice. From one perspective, for instance, the use of a third-party infrastructure or delivery system reduces the bank's control, creates additional constraints on the product and reduces the rewards of successful market penetration. At the same time, the use of a third party reduces sunk costs and thereby increases manoeuvrability in the future. The Bank of Scotland, for instance, might argue that, while the Prestel Gateway system constrained the kind of product it could offer, it was nevertheless able to gain early entry into the market and to do so at a cost which did not limit its future room for manoeuvre.

Getting the right balance between these factors is clearly problematic, especially as different components of home and office systems may be going through different technological life cycles. In particular, given that the telecommunications infrastructure supporting home and office banking has still not reached maturity, it may make sense for financial service firms to view their current offerings as provisional and to limit investments in those components which are likely to prove dispensable in the future.

Technology diffusion

One of the key lessons learned from initial experience with home and office services – and now being applied by the most recent entrants into the field – is the importance of understanding the rate of *diffusion* of this product innovation (Dover, 1988). Whatever the technical merits of a particular innovation, its diffusion will depend largely upon the way it interacts with the established social and economic status quo in a particular sector.

Technical and attitudinal factors (Rogers, 1962) such as compatibility with existing values and systems, the complexity and communicability of the product and its 'divisibility' – i.e. the ease with which consumers can try it out – are likely to exert a significant influence on adoption rates. In other words, the easier it is for potential consumers to understand and experiment with an innovatory product, the more likely it is that they will do so. Conversely, if a new product is hard to understand, more costly and not readily available 'off the shelf' then it will need to have a very powerful advantage over existing products to appeal to more than an idiosyncratic minority of consumers.

This is not to discount the potential diffusion of more radical innovations: all innovations are necessarily taken up initially by smallish groups of early adopters who may also be opinion leaders. Over time, heightened consumer awareness and increasing economies of scale in production can significantly lower the attitudinal and economic constraints on diffusion. Unfortunately, in the early stages of an innovation's life it is practically impossible to distinguish between the small consumer splash from which many ripples flow and the one which means 'sunk without trace'.

Technological trends are little help in arriving at this judgement. For instance, in the late 1970s, one consulting firm predicted that screen-based home banking would be accepted by 45 per cent of all US households by 1985. Following the trend of expectations, huge sums of money – something of the order of $600 million – were invested in this technology by US financial institutions. Yet by the late 1980s only 100,000 people out of a US population of around 200 million had actually adopted home banking technology.

This kind of diffusion issue is very apparent in the emerging segmentation of home and office services. Initial attempts to market screen- and viewdata-based services to personal customers quickly discovered that the advantages offered by home banking did not outweigh the much greater expense and technical complexity involved.

Indeed, it is worth asking just what the costs and benefits of such a system would be to the provider as well as to the personal customer. On the provider's side, many of the most important income-generating services cannot be delivered through such a system. On the other hand, for the customer the potential benefits – extended control of personal bank accounts, the financial gains from the manipulation of balances, ease of bill payment – are compromised because the service is not self-sufficient and free-standing. Cash withdrawals, non-standard payments and access to specialist banking services all demand access to systems outside the scope of home banking: ATMs, cheque books, bank branches and so on. By multiplying contact points with the bank, they reduce the convenience and control afforded by home banking and prevent the customer becoming locked into this particular mode of delivery.

Table 3.4 Constraints on the diffusion of home banking in the UK and USA

Feature	Constraint
Relative advantage (the degree to which an innovation is superior to the ideas it supersedes)	Initial start-up cost: over £100, or $900
Compatibility (the degree to which an innovation is consistent with existing values and past experience)	Lack of a dominant technical standard, fear of obsolescence
Complexity (the degree to which an innovation is difficult to understand or use)	Technophobia, perceived complexity
Divisibility (the degree to which an innovation may be tried on a limited basis)	Limited divisibility, given infrastructural connections
Communicability (the degree to which the results of an innovation may be communicated to others)	Complex decision-making process, concern over ease of use and security

Source: Dover (1988).

In contrast, for the small business users who have now become the major target for screen-based services, not only are the relative advantages of such a product all the greater given their greater need for financial control, but the constraints on use may be reduced by greater technical literacy or possession of a personal computer. The banks too have a greater interest in the individual business person and are more willing to underwrite or customise the product to the individual's needs.

Technology trajectories

One way of viewing home and office services is to see them as part of a general post-war trend (Gershuny, 1978), in which technological and infrastructural innovations turn personal services into products. The washing machine, the vacuum cleaner and the television are all examples of this trend.

In this perspective, the kinds of service currently targeted at small business users are the forerunners of mass-market products of the future which will effectively give each individual a bank in his or her home, in the same way that the washing machine creates a laundry in the home, or the television is the domestic equivalent of the cinema.

The major barriers to such a development are already apparent from our earlier discussion, however. The full range of financial services involves a *two-way* flow of information. It requires a much more elaborate infrastructure than is needed for *one-way* information flows such as television. In addition, the heterogeneity of the information flows makes it difficult to automate any but the most standardised forms of interaction with customers. They are limited to products based on one-way information disclosure – account balance information, the ability to make regular payments, transfer sums between accounts and so on. Automating an extensive range of non-standard services and customer interactions is beyond the capabilities even of state-of-the-art technology. This helps to explain First Direct's decision to accept the added financial costs of around 240 human operators to staff its round-the-clock phone banking service.

The experience of home and office services to date suggests that attempting to forecast their development in purely technological terms is unlikely to be fruitful. Although the initial innovation was hailed as a technological leap forward, subsequent developments have involved a move away from the 'technological fix' towards products differentiated by market segments. Two major segments have been identified: small and medium-sized businesses where various screen-based (PC or viewdata) products meet a need for something less than corporate cash management and treasury services but something more than the standard retail service; and the mass personal market, which has actually seen retrograde moves in technological terms as screen-based products are increasingly swamped by phone-based variants.

Although some crude forms of market segmentation are emerging and the market is no longer driven by technological innovation alone, there is still a tremendous diversity in the home and office products currently on offer. This reflects uncertainty about the appropriate forms of product differentiation more than it does any underlying sets of preferences in the marketplace. It seems likely to be some time before this market matures and dominant products emerge.

CONCLUSIONS

The strategic importance of IT in financial services is heightened by structural features of the sector, particularly the centrality of information processing. But equally important are some of the economic and cultural constraints on the use of IT – notably, the limits on product differentiation and the importance of infrastructures.

The strategic impact of IT – and the return on IT investments – is mediated by the problems of assembling products, delivery systems and infrastructures.

The example of home and office services shows the uncertainty attendant on the pursuit of strategic goals through IT. Moreover, aside from product innovations, a good deal of IT expenditure is allocated to back-office and payment system investments which have little competitive effect.

Chapter 4

Information technology in the financial services sector

Rob Procter

This chapter outlines the use of information technology (IT) in the financial services sector. It begins with a survey of current applications, and goes on to describe some of the more significant new applications now beginning to make an impact. The efficient support of applications requires the provision of appropriate hardware and software environments, the so-called IT infrastructure. The technologies currently in use are described, together with the technical developments necessary to meet the performance requirements of discernible application trends. Knowledge of the technology, and of its developmental trajectory, has become increasingly vital for anyone wishing to understand the implications in a sector which is already almost totally reliant on IT.

CURRENT APPLICATIONS OF IT

The financial services sector is often cited as an example of an industry whose success depends almost entirely on its abilities to acquire, manage and analyse information. It is hardly surprising, therefore, that the sector has been in the forefront of developments and applications of IT. The financial services sector is the largest business user of IT, a position it has held for more than a decade. It is estimated that IT accounts for as much as 20 per cent of expenditure by banks, and probably ranks as their second-largest business cost. Worldwide, financial sector purchases of IT were worth more than $8 billion in 1988, and are expected to nearly double in value by 1994. A vast industry now exists to supply its needs, of which IBM is by some way the largest member – a position it has maintained since the beginning of electronic data processing in the early 1950s.

The role of IT is changing rapidly throughout the corporate sector. The past ten years have witnessed the emergence of a new generation of computer-based office information systems. Tools such as word-processors and desk-top publishing, spreadsheets, electronic mail, databases and decision support systems are now indispensable throughout the corporate workplace, and their impact is being felt at all levels. The following are some of the currently most important IT-based applications and services in the financial sector.

Automated inter-bank payment systems

SWIFT (Society for Worldwide Interbank Financial Telecommunications) is the multinational inter-bank messaging system, developed and owned by its member institutions. SWIFT is responsible for international inter-bank payments. Thousands of billions of pounds' worth of payments are handled by SWIFT daily.

CHAPS (Clearing House Automated Payments System) is the UK counterpart of SWIFT. It is managed by APACS (Association for Clearing Payments Services), which is jointly owned by the clearing banks. Together, CHAPS and SWIFT constitute the core of the modern national and international banking system.

Customer information systems

Accounts databases are used to keep track of customers' balances, transaction histories, etc. They are the cornerstone of both internal operations and external services, providing rapid, interactive access to vital business data. The use of personal computers and communications networks has led to company-wide accessibility, regardless of location. Future applications and services will depend heavily upon the ability of the sector's members to exploit customer information in new ways.

Decision support systems

Credit scoring is a way of computing an individual's creditworthiness. It is based upon a statistical profile of customers' financial behaviour and personal circumstances. Applicants' details are compared with the profile, which is then used as a predictor of risk. New so-called 'intelligent' methods are now increasingly used to supplement the statistical information.

Computer-based financial models are used to analyse and predict business conditions and trends, and provide information for share traders and investment fund managers.

Customer services

EFTPOS (electronic funds transfer at point of sale) is a card-based, automated retail payments system. Customer accounts may be debited immediately on verification and authorisation, or overnight as payment instructions are forwarded from the retailer's system to the banks. EFTPOS has been the subject of much speculation in recent years; technically, it has been feasible for some time. Now, in the UK, it is finally beginning to make the predicted impact. There are two main UK systems: Switch, which is owned by a consortium of banks and building societies, and Barclays' Connect.

ATMs (automated teller machines) were the first example of what is now a growing range of customer-operated services. The success of ATMs has taken the sector by surprise; their original role was merely to provide a cash service out of normal branch hours. To capitalise on the popularity of ATMs, new functions have subsequently been added. These include account balance querying, statements, and cheque book requests. In the long term, ATM services may achieve the convenience of the telephone – a global network, accessible from virtually any location.

Home banking provides direct customer manipulation of accounts through a personal customer interface, which is linked to the bank systems via the telephone network. This is the ultimate in self-service, out-of-hours banking, which looks set to make a significant impact. Costs have now been lowered by the development of telephone handset-based interfaces which utilise the keypad, or even voice, to select services.

Smart cards are the next generation of charge, credit and cash cards. The advantage of the smart card over the magnetic strip card is its greater information storage capacity. The magnetic strip has very limited capacity and cannot be updated once it has been issued. The smart card, however, can hold details of accounts, balances, past transactions, account and service limits, etc., all of which can be updated when the need arises. It also makes it possible to merge the functions of all the different cards into one.

Undoubtedly, all the IT applications and services described above have had a beneficial impact on the operational costs of the sector. ATMs, EFTPOS and home banking, for example, are reducing the numbers of cheques issued, which translates into an immediate saving in handling costs. The long-term benefits, however, lie in the way that IT can change the delivery and the form of financial services. IT provides companies in the sector with the means to compete in new markets at low cost. Home banking systems, for example, have enabled a UK building society to move into banking, and a Scottish bank to gain a foothold in England, without having to invest in the traditional, costly branch infrastructure. IT also provides the key to competing in existing markets with new services.

IT INFRASTRUCTURE

The fundamental role of IT is to facilitate the capture, processing and distribution of information. Advances in IT have not necessarily addressed all of these aspects at once, or in equal measure, however. Meeting the requirements of a large, dispersed organisation, such as a bank, calls for the creation of an IT infrastructure, built from an appropriate blend of the available technologies and system components. Because of its operational importance, change in the infrastructure is more gradual than in some of the component parts; evolution is the sector's preferred strategy to achieve performance improvement without disruption.

The evolution of IT infrastructure in the financial services sector has passed through several phases since the first introduction of computing in the 1950s. With falling hardware costs, head office mainframes have been gradually complemented by the installation of minicomputers at local sites such as bank branches, and finally by personal computers in virtually every branch and office. To ensure maximum reliability, hardware which supports critical services such as accounts databases is now often duplicated. The proliferation of computing resources improved information-processing capacity, but created a potential threat to information distribution as long as they remained in relative isolation from one another. Digital communications networks have become a vital component of the infrastructure, restoring accessibility of information and providing the platform for the integration of applications and services.

But the infrastructures within organisations are also shaped by the sectoral features described in Chapter 3. The banks, for example, must daily reconcile transfers of funds; ATMs are developing into a generic service, whose accessibility is virtually independent of the point of use; retailer systems need to be able to interact with many of the major bank and building society systems to clear EFTPOS and credit card transactions. The progress of integration, at both the organisational and sectoral levels, depends heavily upon the willingness of the members of the IT industry to reach agreement on standards for hardware, software and basic services like communications.

APPLICATIONS OF IT IN MANAGEMENT

In the first phase of corporate IT use, the emphasis was on replacing human effort in the performance of routine, clerical tasks. The classic example is the transaction-processing system, typically involving operations such as payroll, accounts and inventory control. Management began to exploit IT directly with the introduction of management information systems (MISs), which harnessed the information collation and processing capabilities of transaction-processing systems and databases to provide management with regular reports and summaries of business activity. For management, the chief gains accrue from the increased scope for monitoring, controlling and planning of operational procedures which MISs afford. These are important – but none the less routine – management tasks; the operational decision-making environment is predictable in nature, and the problems are well structured and routine. Through increasing the quality and timeliness of information, the principal impact of MISs has been to improve line management productivity, without fundamentally changing the nature of its activities. The speed of decision making has been increased, but the range of options from which decisions must be selected – the search space – remains essentially unaltered.

The availability of MISs might well ensure that the sheer lack of data should never impede decision making, but if used thoughtlessly they can often exacerbate management's problems rather than solve them. Early examples of MISs were often more accurately termed 'management misinformation systems' because so little of the data they provided was really usable.

In this new phase, management applications have been targeted at supporting the decision-making process more directly. For middle and senior management, decision making generally loses its routine and predictable nature; problems are increasingly ill-structured, and the outcomes of decisions uncertain. Decision making takes on more of the characteristics of a heuristic search within a problem space whose limits are ill-defined. These characteristics are exemplified by strategic decision making, by virtue of its distant time horizons, and the inherent difficulty of predicting the moves of other actors in the marketplace.

Decision support systems

In the IT market, confusion over the meaning of terminology is not uncommon. Decision support systems (DSSs), however, seem to be particularly prone to this problem. Freyenfeld's (1984, p. 8) definition is better than most:

> A decision support system is an interactive data processing and display system which is used to *assist* in a *concurrent* decision making process, and which also conforms to the following characteristics:
>
> * it is sufficiently *user-friendly* to be used by the decision maker(s) *in person*,
> * it displays information in a *format* and *terminology* which is familiar to its user(s),
> * it is selective in its provision of information and *avoids* exposing its users(s) to an *information overload*.

The spreadsheet was perhaps the first example of a DSS to achieve widespread use. It provides a simple way of modelling many different kinds of problem – not just financial – and exploring the implications of different decisions. The spreadsheet concept was originally conceived by a Harvard MBA student, and its immediate success undoubtedly owed much to the fact that its problem-solving style and user interface were intuitively obvious to financial sector users and accountants.

Expert systems

Expert systems are probably the best-known example of a new generation of DSSs which are among the first commercial spin-offs from research into artificial intelligence (AI). As their name implies, expert systems attempt to reproduce the problem-solving behaviour of the human expert. Their early promise has not been entirely fulfilled – as with a number of other AI technologies (e.g. speech input and output), their introduction has been accompanied by rather inflated expectations. In the past five years, however, expert systems have begun to penetrate in a big way into corporate decision making, with the financial services sector, as before, leading the way.

An expert system contains a collection of facts, much like a conventional database. What it has that a conventional database lacks is a set of rules which specify how those facts are to be interpreted. These rules represent the distillation of expertise harvested from consultations with acknowledged experts in a particular domain. Together, the facts and rules constitute what is known as the *knowledge base* for a particular problem domain. When posed a problem by the user, the expert system applies the rules to the knowledge base to find a solution, possibly prompting the user for additional evidence as it proceeds.

Practically all the major financial service institutions have expert systems in use or under development. The applications involved include the following:

- Assessment of insurance and credit risks.
- Personal tax and pension planners.
- Market forecasting.
- The management of investment portfolios.
- Detection of abnormal stock price movements.

In the case of investment, it is in asset allocation that they have shown the greatest potential, providing portfolio managers with the means to explore various strategies. A somewhat more dubious example of expert system use is to be found in program trading systems, a practice which has achieved some notoriety since the stock market crash of October 1987. These expert systems automatically buy and sell shares on criteria defined by prices and other market indicators. During the 1987 crash, Wall Street was forced to pull the plug on them for fear that they were actually accelerating the fall in the value of shares. It has since been argued that this move was itself a mistake, and that left to themselves the program traders would have helped to soften the fall.

Neural networks

Neural networks are the latest technology to emerge from AI research and development. It has long been argued that the easiest way to duplicate human reasoning capabilities – and hence intelligent behaviour – is simply to duplicate the structure of the human brain itself; the desired behaviour will then simply emerge as a consequence of the structure. Neural networks (also known as connectionist computing) attempt to copy the essential features of the brain's structure. The architecture of the brain, of course, differs radically from that of conventional computers. The latter are serial machines, processing a stream of instructions and data in strict order, one instruction at a time. The brain, on the other hand, has a massively parallel architecture, consisting of hundreds of billions of relatively simple processing elements, known as neurons.

While in practice the resemblance is more metaphorical than real, the behaviour of neural networks reveals numerous similarities with that of the brain. In particular, rather than being programmed like conventional computers and expert systems, neural network-based systems must be 'trained' to reproduce the required behaviour. In the training process, examples of inputs and their desired outputs are presented to the network, which 'learns' how to match them up. It then becomes capable of producing the correct outputs when presented with new inputs.

The applications that appear to be best suited to neural network techniques are those where codifiable expertise is unavailable and largely intuitive decision-making methods appear to dominate. They are typified by decisions whose resolution involves pattern matching, the ability to recognise an instance as belonging to a particular class, and optimisation, where the best (or near-optimal) decision must be found from a large number of potential candidates. Conventional computer architectures and algorithmic approaches do not perform very well with these kinds of problem, but arguably these are characteristic of many important decision-making situations in financial services.

Among the applications of neural networks being investigated is direct marketing. One example is the selection from bank databases of clients who would be most likely to take up new products and services. The financial profiles of known good clients are used to train the network to recognise the underlying common pattern. Then the network is used to identify other clients whose profiles match the pattern. Results are said to be very promising and better than any other techniques tried so far. Other possible applications in financial services include securities trading, credit approval systems, credit card fraud detection, portfolio selection and evaluation, and market monitoring and forecasting.

Security is another possible future application for neural networks. The financial sector is very aware of the inadequacies of the PIN (personal identity number) as a verification method. Neural networks might be trained to recognise unique physical attributes of customers, such as finger and voice prints, and even signatures.

Both expert systems and neural networks may also be applied to the problem of information overload. A recent study found that senior executives in large institutions may receive as many as 1,000 messages a week from all sources.

The problem is most in evidence in financial services, where the growth of on-line news and information services, such as the Reuters stock market price feed, has been quite dramatic in recent years. The task of extracting relevant information from such sources is becoming impossible for the unaided human user. The standard computer-assisted retrieval technique of key word searches, however, often proves to be unsatisfactory, because the methods for defining the target information are too simplistic; too much irrelevant, or too little relevant, information is usually the result.

Expert system and neural network techniques are being actively evaluated in the quest for effective information retrieval tools. The expert system approach, for instance, applies natural language reasoning and a topic-specific knowledge base to filter out irrelevant information. In the neural network approach, the system is trained to recognise relevant information from examples of the kind of information the user would – and would not – like to see. In trials of these so-called intelligent filters, retrieval precision rates of better than 90 per cent have been reported.

Problems and pitfalls of DSS

In spite of their increased use, the effectiveness of DSSs remains open to question. Numerous studies have shown that their use often results in little real improvement in decision-making performance. Given the number of expert systems that are in use today, surprisingly few success stories are convincingly documented in the literature; in the case of neural networks, there is, currently none. This situation may be explained in part by the reluctance of institutions to reveal information that might jeopardise a competitive advantage. One of the few exceptions to this inconclusive picture is American Express's Authorizer's Assistant, an expert system used to support decision making about charges to a card-holder's account. It is reported to have resulted in an improvement of credit authorisation decisions by 11 per cent, raising the level of correct decisions from 85 per cent to 96 per cent. On the whole, however, the conclusion would seem to be that expert system development may be very costly, and it is often almost impossible to quantify the benefits by conventional measures.

The difficulties of building successful expert systems have been grossly underestimated. The objectives for employing the technology have often been unclear, and the complexity of applications has been misjudged. What has been assumed to be a straightforward development project has often uncovered serious gaps in understanding that can be properly tackled only by research. Financial services were initially regarded as an ideal area for the exploitation of expert system techniques, and the sector has invested heavily in the technology. A 1988 survey indicated that almost 50 per cent of UK insurance companies were using expert systems, and over half of the banks were either using them or in the process of developing them.

More recently, however, a series of setbacks has led the sector to take a rather more cautious view. A typical example of the problems encountered can be found in ARIES (Alvey Research into Insurance Expert Systems), a government-initiated research project, funded by financial services institutions. This succeeded in producing prototype expert systems for insurance risk assessment and investment portfolio management. TAURUS, a follow-up project which was aimed at turning these prototypes into working systems, was not completed. The cause of its failure lies in the nature of investment management decision making. The knowledge it calls upon has been found to be too broad to meet the key criterion of domain specificity. There are signs that, as a result of painful lessons like this, the financial sector is now taking a more pragmatic approach and is beginning to get better results.

There is no doubt, for instance, that expert systems may have a significant impact on organisational competitiveness and the market for products. In financial planning, the use of expert systems is reported to have cut the time needed to prepare a plan for an individual client from between 40 and 80 hours, to less than 10. Now that this service is conceivably within the reach of people with much lower incomes than was previously the case, what was a custom market may have the potential to be transformed into a mass market. The possible business rewards of a bigger market may be counterbalanced, however, by increased competition for business. If expertise is a barrier for firms wanting to enter this or any other market, then expert systems can almost certainly lower it. After all, the great promise of expert systems is that, once captured, the cost of knowledge transfer is negligible.

As a final comment on this topic, it is worth noting that IT applications in this area are still the subject of intense debate. It remains to be seen whether 'intelligent' decision-making tools can serve as complete replacements for human beings, or merely as their assistants. In practice, the answer is likely to depend upon the type of situation into which the technology – be it expert systems or neural networks – is being introduced. The demands of portfolio management, for example, are quite different from those of security trading. For financial services, therefore, the difficult task is not the choice of technology itself. Rather it is specifying those elements of financial decision making which could or should be automated, and those which require human guidance and intervention.

ADVANCES IN DATABASE SYSTEMS

A database is a generalised, structured and integrated collection of data. Operationally, its role is to provide an efficient and secure environment for data collection, maintenance and retrieval. Financial services databases are very important resources, and so high reliability and availability is essential.

A major influence behind the changing role of the database is the realisation of its potential value in the cross-selling of products and services. For example, many financial sector databases contain customer information of great commercial value, such as purchasing patterns and uptake of financial products. Marketing departments can use this information to identify customers who might be interested in a specific product or service. In this way, marketing tools such as direct mail can be targeted more precisely – and hence more efficiently – with the confidence that response rates will be increased. An equally important application area for financial services lies in the identification of markets for new products and services.

Unlocking this latent resource, however, has proved to be extremely difficult and expensive. Many financial sector institutions are handicapped by ageing and inflexible database systems. Often their data is not efficiently structured or integrated for applications which were simply not anticipated when the databases were created. Costly reorganisation may be the only effective answer. Customer information provides a typical illustration of the problems. Following traditional financial services practice, its databases have been structured around bank accounts or insurance policies, rather than the marketing concept of the customer. As a result, information about any single customer may be scattered across several different accounts, databases and even physical systems, making collation impractical or even impossible. From a marketing viewpoint, it is clear that account-oriented databases are poorly suited to building up profiles of current customers. What is even worse is that they are also of little use for keeping track of potential customers: by definition, account-oriented databases contain information only about existing account holders.

Moreover, many of the new database applications require more than a reorganisation of existing data to ensure their success. Conventional computer filing systems are not able to meet such a stringent set of requirements. They need better hardware to meet the increased transaction loads, but most important, they need more sophisticated tools for data management – specialist software tools, which are known collectively as a Database Management System, or DBMS.

When a large collection of data is being shared between many users, then it is inevitable that sometimes their activities, and the database transactions they initiate, will be in conflict. The DBMS arbitrates between transactions when conflicts arise, and determines a safe order for their execution. Guaranteeing conflict-free query processing while maintaining high transaction performance requires considerable sophistication. In fact, for many financial sector applications 100 per cent reliability is an operational necessity. This requires systems to be designed for a high degree of fault tolerance, and to be able to maintain a service even if a major component, such as a mainframe, fails. Most banks, for example, duplicate their principal on-line database systems, so that when one fails the other can take over automatically.

With the development of increasingly large and complex database applications came the need to formalise the description of the data. It was met by the introduction of the *data model*, a set of conceptual and operational tools for describing the database contents, its logical structure and basic properties. The Codasyl (Committee on Data System Languages) or *network* data model was the first for which an industry-wide standard was defined. Most first-generation, commercial DBMS products have been based either on this or on the *hierarchical* model typified by IBM's IMS database. Since the early 1980s, however, a new generation of DBMSs have begun to make a major commercial impact. The increasing preference among financial sector users for these new DBMSs is an unmistakable sign of the database's changing role.

Databases typically have long lives, and their contents are subject to constant update. Change always carries with it the danger of corruption and the undermining of data integrity, i.e. a loss of accuracy or correctness. For example, invalid updates might be caused by incorrect data entry, or by errors in other application software that accesses the database contents. Automatic integrity checking requires a more sophisticated form of data model which can specify sets of rules defining valid updates. In their simplest form, integrity constraints may just define a range of permissible values for a particular data item. The DBMS can then check updates against the range of values and reject those which do not comply.

Integrity constraints are one way to incorporate more of the semantics of the data (i.e. its meaning) into the description of the database contents. Incorporating semantics is vital if databases are to become more oriented to business needs. Of course, by its nature the problem of capturing data semantics can never be wholly solved. It is entirely possible, however, to create data-modelling tools which are better suited to the database's new roles. Capturing semantics is the key for the eventual metamorphosis from database to information base.

Relational databases

In the relational database, the contents are represented as a collection of tables, which are known as relations. Each relation denotes a distinct data type in the database. In a typical bank database, these might be 'Customers' and 'Accounts'. The relation's contents consist of a number of rows and columns. Each row represents a specific instance of a relation, and the columns represent its attributes. The attributes of Customer might be *Name*, *Account Number* and *Address*, and those of Account *Account Number*, *Type*, *Balance* and *Overdraft Limit*. A database will typically contain many relations, one for each data type in the database description or *schema*. By means of shared attributes, relations can be linked together to capture the relationships between them, e.g. the ownership of an account by a customer. These can then be used to retrieve data from several different relations.

In hierarchical and network data models, data relationships are represented by embedded links, thus tying them closely to the underlying storage mechanisms. The great advance of the relational data model has been to separate the data model from the storage. It means that database designers and implementors do not need to know the physical details of how or where the data is stored. They are left free to think about the database purely in terms of its logical structure. For the organisation, this makes it easier to ensure that a good match between the logical structure, business and user requirements is obtained.

There can be little doubt that such features have had a major bearing on the popularity of the relational model, even though none of the present commercial offerings fully implements the original concept. In financial services, in particular, the relational DBMS is becoming the default option. Among the major contenders in the relational database market are IBM's DB2, Oracle Corporation's Oracle, and Relational Technology's Ingres. DB2 has been installed in over 5,000 sites worldwide and is currently the sector leader.

Object-oriented databases

The need to cut database development times and reduce maintenance and administration costs on the one hand, and to cope with more complex applications on the other, has exposed weaknesses in relational DBMSs. As a consequence, the financial services sector is already looking at new types of DBMS, and in particular at *object-oriented* databases (OODBs), which are derived from object-oriented programming (OOP) concepts. For the database implementor, OODBs offer a number of important advantages. They support incremental change and improve the reusability of existing software, providing benefits throughout all phases of the database life cycle.

These advantages mostly derive from the concepts of *class* and *inheritance*. Every object in an OODB is a member of a class, which defines its type and hence its properties. Inheritance allows classes to share properties and new classes to be created from existing ones. For example, the class 'Customer' might be defined as an aggregation of the classes 'Current Account', 'Deposit Account', 'Mortgage', etc., while the class 'Employee' might be defined as the generalisation of the classes 'Branch Manager', 'Teller', 'Ledger Clerk', etc.

Class and inheritance together create a powerful tool for capturing the semantics of data. It reduces information redundancy and encourages code reuse, and so helps to reduce implementation and maintenance effort. The combination of these features makes OODBs the best solution yet for the design of complex databases and for the management of changes in data, and database structure, over long periods of time.

The impact of OODBs on the sector is, however, open to question. The current lack of an industry standard is a disincentive to switch technologies at the present time. By adding inheritance to the relational model, the *extended* relational database achieves many of the benefits of the object-oriented approach. Given present financial sector trends, the extended relational database may prove a more viable development route.

Hypertext databases

At present, only 5 per cent of all corporate data is stored on computer systems. Even in the financial services sector, with its large-scale use of databases, paperless information handling remains a remote objective. The traditional database is best suited to managing large collections of homogeneous, highly structured data, i.e. collections of items, each of a single type, which are interrelated in relatively simple ways. In reality, however, not all data fall into this category; in fact, much corporate data is heterogeneous, with complex interrelationships, and so has remained paper-bound.

In hypertext databases, the contents are organised as a multi-dimensional network of interconnected information nodes. The user can browse around the nodes at will, moving from one to another by traversing any of the many built-in links. Hypertext, therefore, can fill the gap in corporate data storage and management services. In the longer term, it may also serve as the basis for company-wide information networks.

Auditing is one application of hypertext which is of particular interest to financial services. The auditing process produces large quantities of documentation that typically contain a wide range of interrelated information, which is inherently heterogeneous, non-linear and complex. The present procedures for handling this information are, in effect, a manual hypertext system. It has been estimated that up to 30 per cent of the time required to complete an audit is spent on the preparation, maintenance and review of the documentation. A computer-based hypertext audit system has the potential to improve access to information, and to cut costs by reducing the time and effort necessary for document production and maintenance.

DISTRIBUTED SYSTEMS

Advances in hardware have encouraged the emergence of a range of distinctive computing environments. The falling costs and rising performance first of minicomputers, and later of personal computers, have made them an increasingly attractive financial option to the central, time-sharing mainframe. Cheap computing power has enabled the financial sector to introduce IT into the branches, initially with minicomputer-based, batch back-office administration systems. The next stage has been to provide branch networks and personal computers, giving staff on-line, interactive access to central databases, and customers self-service banking.

The mainframe concept was born at a time when processor cycles were expensive. Now they are cheap, and are continuing to fall in price by a factor of 50 per cent every two years. The trends now favour the use of a number of small computers rather than one large, central, time-sharing mainframe. The cost of processing on a single-user workstation is about one-tenth that of a minicomputer, which itself is about one-third the cost of mainframe processing. Many applications, including the major relational database products, have now migrated on to these cheaper computing platforms. Replacing the mainframe with a collection of personal computers can reduce capital investment dramatically, often by a factor of ten or more. Even more significantly, it can also cut running costs. Organisations have discovered that the number of technical staff needed to support this kind of computing environment is often much smaller than a mainframe would require. Sales of mainframe computers to the financial services sector are expected to fall from a figure of 50 per cent by value in 1984, to 25 per cent by 1994. In contrast, sales by value of personal computers are expected to rise from less than 20 per cent to more than 40 per cent over the same period.

The rationale for distributed systems is to provide computing resources to match all requirements, maximise their utilisation and enable users to co-operate and exchange data freely. The aim is to regain the advantages of centralised time-sharing computer systems – their ease of sharing information, and the availability of large amounts of computing power when needed – while retaining the benefits of personal computers, their speed of response, and their power to drive user-friendly graphical interfaces which have become crucial for the successful adoption of IT by a wider (and less computer-literate) user community. The distributed system concept reveals the mainframe-versus-personal-computer dichotomy, so often featured in the IT press, to be falsely conceived; their strengths are complementary. Far from being on the brink of extinction, the mainframe will continue to have a role in financial sector IT for as long as there are large, complex applications which make heavy demands on processing resources.

The fully distributed system architecture is still some way off. As a first step, the so-called client/server architecture is gaining favour. The strategy is to split basic system services and application processing between a front-end machine (the client) and a back-end machine (the server), and to connect them together through a high-speed communications network. The front-end is usually a personal computer or workstation, and is dedicated to one single user. One of the front-end's roles is to perform any processing that can be done locally, thereby relieving the back-end machine of some of the load. The back-end, which might be a mainframe or a specialised database machine, provides the service required. Apart from its cheapness, one of the reasons why the client/server architecture is finding acceptance is because the front-end has the local hardware and processing power necessary for graphical displays. This is essential to provide applications with the kind of user-friendly interface more appropriate for the less experienced user.

COMMUNICATIONS

Modern IT is the result of the integration of computing and communications: as communications have become indispensable to computing, so computing has become indispensable to communications. High-performance, high-capacity communications networks are the backbone of distributed systems. Adding processing capability to networks provides the basis for better communications by improving their reliability and performance. In the past, the rate of improvement in communications technology performance has not matched the pace set by computing. Attempts to introduce distributed system concepts in the 1970s failed because of the inadequacies of the communications technologies of the time. This imbalance in progress is now being remedied with the advent of new digital communications technologies and standards. With deregulation now set to allow other operators to compete in the communications market, costs should fall even more quickly.

New digital communications technologies and networks have led to increased information-carrying capacity, reduced costs and improved reliability. They have made it feasible for the financial services sector to build the infrastructure required for the integration of head office and branch systems, and for new customer services, such as ATMs, EFTPOS, teleshopping and home banking. A new network-based service recently introduced uses a technique known as data broadcasting. Information on stolen cheque and credit cards can be broadcast nationwide in a few seconds by utilising the spare capacity in domestic TV signals.

The proliferation of services has been matched by an increase in the number of networks. Currently, different networks have been established for ATMs, EFTPOS and other services; some of the larger financial sector organisations have as many as ten or more different networks. Network integration is highly desirable if the sector is to reduce costs. The communications strategy of large users, such as the clearing banks, has been to establish their own proprietary intra-organisational data networks. Networks supporting inter-organisational services such as CHAPS and SWIFT, however, are integrated at the sector level, and this strategy may well be adopted for ATM and EFTPOS networks in the future.

The growing importance of communications to the financial sector is underlined by its increasing share of the IT budget, and the recognition that there is a new set of problems to be tackled. Demand for information-carrying capacity is growing rapidly, and the importance of reliability has never been greater. Meeting these requirements calls for the attention of specialist personnel to monitor performance, manage networks and plan future expansion and services, tasks which are becoming increasingly complex. In line with recent trends in other branches of IT, many financial sector institutions may be expected to turn to third-party service providers to supply and manage their networks, rather than try to do it themselves, in-house.

OPEN SYSTEMS

Distributed systems highlight the importance of standards to the successful development and marketing of new technologies. IT standards define the extent to which a single – and indeed all – manufacturer's products can work together. Without agreed hardware and software interfaces between the different system components, distributed systems would remain a paper concept. Some of the most significant advances in communications of the last ten years have centred around the defining of standards, rather than the development of new technologies. For IT, the establishment of standards can often be just as important as improvements in performance.

In some cases, IT standards have been the result of formal negotiations between the interested parties – principally manufacturers and users – orchestrated by institutions such as ISO (International Standards Organisation). This planned process has often been complemented by informal market mechanisms – the domination by one particular manufacturer, or overwhelming market preference. As the largest supplier to the financial services sector, IBM has long enjoyed a privileged position; many of its products have become *de facto* standards. This domination is now slipping, however. Other manufacturers have occupied niche markets: Tandem's range of fault-tolerant machines is one example. The sector is also increasingly unwilling to remain locked into one supplier as the technology options continue to widen. Now the development of the *open systems* concept promises to solve their problems. Open systems mean that users will no longer be forced to commit themselves to a single manufacturer when they invest in a new system.

UNIX is emerging as the most likely foundation for the open system standard. UNIX was originally conceived in the early 1970s as an operating system for minicomputers. Over the years it has migrated to mainframes and even personal computers. With its portability, it has already become a *de facto* standard and so is an obvious contender. UNIX is backed by X/Open, which is an international consortium of manufacturers.

SECURITY AND CONFIDENTIALITY

The increased use of IT has created a number of new security problems for the financial services sector. Inevitably, new forms of financial service delivery have opened up new opportunities for crime. In the USA, ATM-based frauds are estimated to have cost the banks $40 million in 1987. This figure will undoubtedly increase as ATMs become as ubiquitous as public telephones. More sophisticated forms of fraud may be perpetrated if access is gained to database and transaction management services. The dangers of this increase as the customer–banking system interface becomes steadily more sophisticated. Home banking is just the beginning of a trend to provide the customer with direct access to the sector's IT systems. In addition to the problem of fraud, there is also the issue of confidentiality of information. Literally, billions of bytes of data flow through the financial system networks on a daily basis, some of them over potentially vulnerable public lines.

In order to guarantee security, the sector's IT systems must resolve the potentially conflicting business requirements of (a) confidentiality – ensuring that information is divulged only to those authorised to see it; (b) integrity – ensuring that only authorised people can change information and gain access to services; and (c) availability – ensuring rapid access to information and services, irrespective of time and distance.

Networks make conventional security measures for systems and data obsolete, and the determined electronic hacker will not be deterred by routine computer security measures such as passwords. Financial services sector institutions are looking with great interest at various biometric techniques for verifying identity, such as fingerprints. Signature verification is another technique currently under investigation. Such methods may prove to be suitable for use with both employees and customers.

Security problems are compounded by the fact that very few, if any, of the present generation of commercial computer systems are engineered to withstand the sophisticated hacker; as recent episodes have convincingly demonstrated, not even military systems are secure. Typically, there are too many 'back-door' ways in for better 'front-door' security methods to provide the complete answer.

The IT industry has now become more alert to security issues, but it will take time for better security measures to come into wide use. User organisations, meanwhile, can take additional protective measures for themselves. The encryption of sensitive data makes it less vulnerable to unauthorised access and is standard practice for services such as SWIFT and CHAPS. Keeping back-up copies of valuable information makes it less vulnerable to malicious damage. Unfortunately, however, hacking is a problem for which there is no guaranteed technical solution; no system will ever be totally invulnerable.

Legislative changes have also made an impact. Since 1984 the Data Protection Act has made it a legal requirement that UK commercial data users take all 'reasonable' precautions against access by unauthorised people, or the malicious corruption of data. The Act has in fact put a brake on the shift from paper to digital data storage, since it defines statutory rights of access for 'data subjects', and penalties for keeping false or out-of-date information. Some banks are finding it more convenient to maintain traditional manual customer files, which are beyond the provisions of the Act. This strategy may prove to be of limited value, however. A draft EC directive, aimed primarily at harmonising data protection laws, is calling for their extension to cover manual files.

IT AND THE USER INTERFACE

That the quality of the user interface – the part of the system that users see and must actually work with – is critical to the success of IT, has become a truism. With the spread of IT, however, the identity of the financial services sector 'user' is becoming rather diffuse.

Ten years ago, 'user' had only one meaning in the financial services sector: a well-defined group of employees, typically clerks and tellers, and perhaps a few managers. Now virtually every employee is a user. This is just one reason why human factors have led to a revision of design priorities. Improving user efficiency is now often more important for successful IT than increasing hardware performance. In the past, training has often been seen as the answer, but now it may no longer be sufficient. Where the use of IT is discretionary, if not completely voluntary – as it may well be within the ranks of senior management, for example – it must be designed to match users' needs and expertise more closely.

The requirement now is for IT-based tools with user interfaces which are easy to learn and easy to use, yet possess the power to assist in the solution of complex problems. Like all ideals, this combination is proving hard to satisfy. Not least of the difficulties is the fact that the optimal interface style can vary quite significantly with the background and experience of the user. This may make it hard to design a single interface which will be acceptable to all of the potential users. The vast majority of the new users are not prepared to immerse themselves in the esoteric lore and jargon of traditional computing in order to do a job. Experience shows that systems and applications must be easy to learn and use, or they will be ignored. Fortunately, much has been learnt in the last ten years about how to design interfaces for the less experienced user, and this technology is now widely available.

Since the launch of the Apple Macintosh and the *direct manipulation* interface concept in 1984, more and more manufacturers have acknowledged its user appeal and copied it – even traditionally staid IBM. Most expert opinion agrees that the direct manipulation interface is the easiest interaction style for the non-technical user. Research seems to confirm that it reduces the likelihood of making mistakes, that the time for users to acquire competence is much shorter, and that skills are retained for longer. Producers of application software are being encouraged to adopt a common interface style in their own products. Users will benefit from the consistency that this standardisation will bring to applications, making it much easier and less time-consuming for them to master new products.

The customer as user

The impact of IT on service delivery means that customers must now be counted among the users of financial services IT. Financial services IT now has a customer interface, which is set to increase in sophistication and complexity as new customer-operated, cash management services appear. Good interface design for this category of user is even more challenging. Among this group, age, education and experience may differ widely. Employees may at least be trained in the use of new technologies, and they have colleagues around who can help them. For the ATM or home banking user, however, training is simply not a viable option. Banks have found it necessary to provide help desks and round-the-clock support staff for home banking systems, which can be an expensive way of dealing with poor interface design. Also, if a customer needs to call the help desk, the damage to customer confidence may well be permanent, even though the specific problem may be successfully dealt with. More generally, it is questionable whether the user relations skills which are applied to in-house users directly translate to the external user: that is, to customers. The latter group greatly extend the possibilities of deliberate or accidental abuse, and IT staff have little control over the way in which the technology is used. This suggests that IT management may need to incorporate greater knowledge of customer behaviour in their development of market-oriented systems.

Ironically, as a direct consequence of the expanding customer–IT system interface, the opportunities for personal contact with the customer are diminishing. This was one of a number of unforeseen impacts of the introduction of ATMs. The quality of service as perceived by the customer is coming more and more to depend upon the technology, rather than the helpfulness of staff. This is actually helping to undermine the kind of personal touch which is one of the most effective means both of maintaining a distinctive image and of selling new services to customers. In the view of many bank branch managers, word of mouth beats direct marketing, and personal networks are more valuable than IT-based ones. One of the hoped-for strategic impacts of IT has been the release of more staff from administration to spend more time talking with the customer; first of all, however, it seems that the sector must find some new incentives to lure customers back into the branches. Alternatively, and rather more radically, these automated forms of service delivery might be used to advertise other services.

PERFORMANCE ISSUES

Though the new roles of IT have led to a shift in technical priorities in the financial sector, the pressure for improved system performance continues unabated. Many of the business and organisationally-oriented developments in IT incur significant performance penalties. The adoption of the relational DBMS, for example, has led to increased processing overheads because database structure is less closely tied to the underlying data storage mechanisms. More complex financial applications, such as knowledge-based decision support systems, also significantly increase processing load. The result has been that the sector has found that many of these applications perform poorly, or are impractical with the current technology.

System performance is still the ultimate constraint on application viability in financial services. It is estimated that the current database performance will need to be improved by a factor of 100 or even more to keep pace with demand. The IT industry has invested a lot of effort in improving the performance of relational databases. As a result, it is estimated that it is increasing at the rate of 30 per cent per year. An increasing number of applications now fall within the capacity of relational DBMS, but the more efficient network DBMS is likely to remain the choice for time-critical transaction processing for some time yet.

When the greater proportion of database transactions are routine, and so can be anticipated, it is possible to tune or optimise data storage structures so that data can be accessed more efficiently. Now, with decision support, management reporting and direct marketing applications becoming an increasing part of the database processing load, the transaction demand has become more unpredictable, and thus difficult – or even impossible – to optimise in this way.

Expert systems have often been one of the casualties of poor database performance. Some of the initial failures and subsequent disillusionment may be attributed to a failure to understand their performance implications. Applications involving realistically complex rule bases have often proved impractical on conventional hardware, and prototype systems have failed to scale up; expert systems for advising on bank loan applications may have more than a thousand rules, and more complex systems may have as many as ten thousand. Wall Street is having to use some of the most powerful supercomputers for its trading systems, financial modelling and portfolio analysis.

The long-term solution to performance problems lies in the development of technologies which are more suited to the new applications. In the future, hardware will need to be optimised for symbolic computation, or 'knowledge processing', rather than data manipulation. Eventually, the 'knowledge engine' will take its place alongside the 'database engine' in the financial sector IT infrastructure. In the meantime, the sector must ensure that applications such as expert systems are properly integrated into the existing IT infrastructure if it is to exploit the benefits of the new applications fully. Technical issues in the form of improved hardware, systems architectures and software will remain high on the list of priorities.

IT INFRASTRUCTURE, SOFTWARE ENGINEERING AND BUSINESS STRATEGY

According to Earl (1989), corporate IT infrastructure consists of four distinct components:

- Computing – the information-processing hardware and system software.
- Communications – the telecommunications networks and protocols for interlinking and interworking.
- Data – the corporate data assets, and the requirements of use, access, control and storage.
- Applications – the corporate applications, and the development methodologies.

Arguably, not all of these components can claim to be strategic for financial services, or even to provide a specific competitive advantage. Many computing and communications technologies, for example, have reached a stage of development where they are available as generic products on the open market. Their form may differ from one corporate context to another only to the extent that, as generic products, they may need some adaptation to meet local requirements. Computing and communications technologies are commonly referred to, therefore, as the core of the IT function; the implicit assumption is that decisions about the core are not problematic, and that they are without strategic import. In this schema, it is corporate data and applications which constitute the strategic component of the IT function; it is these technologies which are used to realise the business concepts, and which can deliver the competitive advantage.

The difficulty with this schema is that it does not address the complex interaction between, on the one hand, the core technology and, on the other, the applications which are built on top of it. The viability of applications may well depend upon the performance of the core technology, which is by no means completely unproblematic. Though the focus of IT policy has shifted to applications, innovation and development continue to change the composition of the core. The range of technical options is steadily growing, with the result that core technology choices may well be difficult to make; at the very least, therefore, core technology decisions must be informed by current application – and hence business – strategy. The problem for many financial service institutions is that the people charged with making decisions about the IT core often lack the necessary business expertise, and vice versa.

Innovations such as the spreadsheet noted earlier illustrate two important lessons for the IT industry: (1) the design of computer-based tools, and especially the user interface, is critical to their acceptance, and (2) non-technical users can make significant contributions to technological development; indeed, they are arguably best placed to do so, having the application and the domain knowledge that is frequently so important to successful innovation – and which developers usually lack. The IT industry faces a major problem because its highly developed division of labour denies it easy access to user expertise. A number of recent developments in software engineering reflect attempts to address this issue.

The IT industry has regularly found itself in a crisis in the last 20 years over its competence to design and deliver systems in time, and that match client needs and expectations. Since the late 1960s, the focus of this problem has been software. In response, the industry has pursued a number of initiatives aimed at improving methodologies and tools for systems design and implementation. Software engineering has been the cumulative result. Yet each stage in the development of software engineering principles has succeeded in alleviating the apparent problems only for new ones to emerge.

For example, in the area of expert systems, one of the major lessons has been the importance of paying attention to user needs. If users are to be active agents in problem-solving tasks, then their requirements must receive the highest priority. An approach to software development is required in which users can participate in a meaningful way. Software engineers must be prepared to use prototyping to discover users' requirements, and to repeat this process perhaps several times. Most important is the need to determine what is the appropriate division of tasks and responsibilities between the system and the user. This is an issue that goes deeper than the look and feel of the user interface; fundamentally, it is a question of job design. Applications like expert systems call for a much more thorough understanding of users' psychology, and of their possible reactions to the technology, than has been evident previously.

The role of IT as a strategic resource, with its implications for competitiveness, presents a new challenge for software engineering. It is now realised that success depends upon business priorities driving IT development, with the requirement that IT expertise be available to decision-makers at the highest levels. Strategic IT also raises questions for the financial services sector's procurement policies, and in particular the role of in-house IT expertise upon which it has traditionally relied. Exploiting the full potential of IT, however, will depend upon the sector achieving a blend of both the old and the new, especially in expertise. For success, strategic IT projects will need to secure effective participation throughout all phases, and at all levels. Ultimately, it is the capacity of financial sector institutions to adapt themselves which holds the key to ensuring that the right expertise is available at the right time, and in the right place.

Chapter 5

Retailer strategies in financial services: UK and international contexts

Steve Worthington

As we indicated in Chapter 2, one of the major strategic issues of recent times has been the move by retailers to enter the financial services market, by issuing their own credit cards, by offering mainstream financial services (e.g. personal loans) or by establishing alternatives to the existing bank-controlled payment systems. Using a variety of international examples, this chapter explores the origins and potential consequences of these strategic initiatives. In particular, it highlights those areas where technological change and new market opportunities have been exploited by retailers, with varying degrees of success.

Given the kind of structural and technological change described in Chapter 2, which is tending to release financial services from the grip of the existing branch infrastructures, while allowing retailers to handle such services through generic technologies such as databases, EPOS (electronic point of sale) and card-processing systems, the success or failure of retailer strategies seems likely to be an important determinant of the future distribution of financial services business.

RETAILER CREDIT CARDS

Already well developed in the United Kingdom, these are attractive to retailers both because of the potential information they reveal about a retailer's customers and because they provide an alternative means of payment to the Visa, MasterCard and Amex cards, etc., on which the retailers must pay merchant service fees.

The UK figures provided by the Retail Credit Group in December 1990 cover some 75 per cent of the total retailer credit market and include such major card issuers as the Burton Group, Marks and Spencer, Next, the House of Fraser, Sears, Storehouse and Dixons. Their figures, shown in Table 5.1, reveal a

Table 5.1 Number of UK Retail Credit Group members' cards in circulation in the United Kingdom 1988–1990 and credit outstanding 1988–1990

	Quarter	Number of accounts (000s)	Credit outstanding (£m)
1988	1	8,506	1,209
	2	8,545	1,184
	3	8,800	1,176
	4	8,522	1,271
1989	1	8,489	1,170
	2	8,871	1,174
	3	8,709	1,172
	4	9,179	1,338
1990	1	9,300	1,271
	2	9,599	1,251
	3	9,534	1,220
	4	9,572	1,362

Source: Retail Credit Group.

steady rise in the number of cards issued, but a flattening out of the level of credit outstanding (debt).

While at first glance these figures might lead the reader to conclude that the retailer credit card has entered the mature stage of the product life cycle, closer analysis points to an even more pronounced 'flattening' of the growth curve. The figures for number of accounts include the Marks and Spencer (M & S) Chargecard which, since its launch in April 1985, has acquired some 2 million accounts, with some 2.5 million cards issued, a very high proportion of which (90 per cent) are active. A great deal of that growth in M & S card numbers occurred during the period covered by the Retail Credit Group's statistics, and their success has disguised the lack of progress being made by some of the other card-issuing members of the Retail Credit Group. The M & S Chargecard is a particularly successful retailer credit card based on the reputation of that retailer and the fact that it is the only credit card accepted in their stores.

Chargecard sales account for over 16 per cent of sales and contributed £5.5 million profit to M & S's results for the year ending 31 March 1989. Some 60 per cent of M & S card-holders pay off their credit accounts in full at the end of each month, and 70 per cent of card-holders are women, with the majority of card-holders being in the 25–44 age bracket. Marks & Spencer also have a full banking licence and they have used their card-holders to launch their personal loan scheme, which has now been extended to the general public. The card-holder list was also used to market the Investment Portfolio, a unit trust from M & S which pulled £5.6 million from investors during its initial three-week offer period in 1988 and a further £10 million later that year.

The macro figures from the Retailer Credit Group do demonstrate that, after years of growth in the number of accounts, the high interest rates of the late 1980s and early 1990s seem to have had a dampening effect on the total amount of credit outstanding and the number of accounts. However, the subsequent decline in retail spending and the associated squeeze of retailer margins will if anything encourage retailers to look at ways of revitalising their store cards so as to secure customer loyalty and maximise customer spending within their own stores. Although there are undoubtedly benefits to be gained for retailers from providing credit – building up customer databases, cross-selling through direct marketing and even diversifying into providing financial services – nevertheless the critical rationale behind a retailer credit card is that it enables retailers to build a 'privileged relationship' with their customers which sustains customer loyalty and, it is hoped, pre-empts a higher proportion of their spending power to the retailer(s) whose card(s) they hold. Burke (1989) provides evidence of retailers' views of this privileged relationship, while Worthington (1990a) discusses how retailers could regenerate their credit cards, particularly in the light of the findings of the Monopolies and Mergers Commission report into card services (1989). For example, they might offer the lower 'cash' price on sales through their store card, under the dual-pricing legislation which came into force in the United Kingdom in March 1991, as a consequence of the Monopolies and Mergers report.

But whatever the current problems facing the retail sector, its continuing importance in this area can be gauged from the fact that there are now some 12 million retail credit cards in circulation in the United Kingdom, with the multiple retailers shown in Table 5.2 being the major players in this particular market.

Other retailers which run their own store cards include Littlewoods, Kingfisher, Rumbelows, Comet, Granada, B & Q and MFI, and even allowing for the bullish claims often associated with retailers, it is not difficult to see where the figure of 12 million comes from. Retailer cards are not, however, as

Table 5.2 Major retail credit card issuers 1989

Retailer	Number of cardholders (millions)
Burton Group	2.60
Marks and Spencer	2.50
House of Fraser	1.75
Next	1.60
John Lewis Partnership	0.80
Sears	0.50
Storehouse	0.50
Dixons	0.50
	10.75

important in the United Kingdom as they are in the USA where retailer cards dwarf bank cards in numbers issued; Sears alone issues 61 million cards and these account for 65 per cent of Sears' sales.

RETAILERS AND FINANCIAL SERVICES

Developments in the USA provide some evidence of the threat that retailer credit cards can pose to the traditional types of financial service provided by the banks. Worthington (1988) describes how Sears in January 1986 launched the Discover card which rivals the usual bank credit cards in that it can be used in a wide variety of locations besides Sears' own stores. The Discover card is now accepted by over 1 million outlets in the retailing and service trades, and there are around 33 million consumers who hold a Discover card. Some 70–80 per cent of Discover card-holders also have a Sears credit card, although this is hardly surprising as holders of a Sears card were the first consumers to be offered a Discover card. The card has been readily accepted by other retailers because the service charges made by Sears are lower than those charged by the other credit card operators such as Visa, MasterCard and American Express. While exact percentage figures are hard to establish, the Discover card charges are believed to be substantially below 2 per cent, while bank card charges in the USA are around 2.2–2.4 per cent and American Express charges are in the range of 3–3.5 per cent, although both these figures would be lower for major store groups.

With the absence of any annual fee (in contrast to the existing USA credit and charge cards), the entitlement to an annual rebate of up to 1 per cent on all purchases made with the card and the reputation of Sears behind it, the Discover card has become a very serious competitor to the existing bank, travel and entertainment cards in the USA. As a major retailer, Sears is also committed to providing financial services other than credit to its retail card-holders and to Discover card-holders. The Discover card is now accepted in 16,000 ATMs in the USA, with transactions running at the rate of 400,000 a month – far more, for example, than Visa itself achieves.

Sears bought the Wall Street firm of Dean Witter Reynolds in 1982 and used that business to establish over 300 in-store financial centres, dealing both in stocks and shares and in real estate under the banner of Coldwell Banker, another subsidiary of Sears. In early 1989 Sears decided that selling 'socks and shares' did not mix and it changed the character of its in-store financial centres from being manned by staff from Dean Witter and Coldwell Banker to being unmanned desks. Help will be given to potential customers in the form of leaflets and pamphlets, and free telephone lines have been installed, linked directly to nearby free-standing offices of the two companies. Sears decided upon this review of its financial services strategy when it realised that a retail store does not necessarily provide the correct ambience for the buying of stocks and shares or real-estate deals.

Sears, however, is not cutting back on its Allstate Insurance offices which trade both within the Sears stores and in free-standing offices. Allstate Insurance operations reported a net income of $815 million for the year ending December 1989, while Dean Witter, which includes the Discover card, reported a net income of $166 million. Sears has had some setbacks in the positioning of its financial service propositions, but the range of financial services that it offers and the level of business that it does, as indicated by the above figures, make Sears a major player not just in retailing but also in the financial services sector, and as such it provides a very real threat to the still fragmented American banks. Legal actions in late 1990 revealed that Sears has ambitions to launch its own Visa credit card, thereby further engaging in head-to-head competition with the existing financial services providers in the USA.

Italy's Benetton Group provided another example of a retailer moving into the provision of financial services, in this case by the provision of a retail 'supermarket' to distribute both its own Benetton brand products and the branded product of leading 'manufacturers' of financial services (Shamoon, 1989).

The Benetton family intended to distribute their financial products independently of their 4,500 quasi-franchised shops worldwide; not to depend on business generated or guaranteed by Benetton and not to capitalise on the Benetton trademark. Their financial services operation was intended, however, to share some of the disciplines and dynamics of the Benetton Group: its entrepreneurial culture in distribution, its philosophy of laying off risk in production and its highly developed target marketing, which is customer-led.

Benetton was to rely on alliances with the specialist providers of financial services, such as the Prudential Corporation, which can quickly assemble the products such as pensions and insurance that Benetton feels its consumers require. Those alliances were also eventually to provide a powerful distribution network both to rival the Italian banking groups and to take advantage of any opportunities that arise from 1992. Benetton's strategy was to develop a distribution network so that European competitors would find it hard to break into the Italian market, and Benetton would then take the best of their products and place them through its own distribution network.

That ease of entry by retailers into financial services is also matched by ease of exit is demonstrated by Benetton's subsequent withdrawal from this market in early 1990. Benetton said that its financial services operations were in need of capital for further development which the family had decided should instead be concentrated on the group's core activities.

In the United Kingdom both Marks and Spencer and the Burton Group have acquired full banking licences to enable them to offer a wide variety of financial services to their customers, and Marks and Spencer in particular have already been successful in bringing financial products to the marketplace. Reference has been made earlier to the personal loans offered by Marks and Spencer, originally only to their credit card-holders but now extended to all customers. The Marks and Spencer Investment Portfolio is the name given to the unit trust which Marks and Spencer launched in 1988, and its success indicates the potential for United Kingdom retailers to offer mainstream financial services – provided, of course, that they have a reputation which the general public feel they can trust!

Marks and Spencer marketed their unit trust by mailing all their credit card-holders as well as 130,000 share-holders and another 300,000 people from a bought-in list. Brochures were also on display at all Marks and Spencer's 280 stores. Although no formal analysis has been carried out, many of the investors are believed to be first-time investors who were attracted by the Marks and Spencer name, one that they know and trust. More than 52,000 applications were received. A total of 39,000 investors made a lump-sum investment averaging £1,400, and 12,500 investors took out regular savings plans with an average payment of £25. The number of investors taking out regular savings plans is unusually high, especially for an initial launch. The company used four main marketing channels: direct mail to its credit card-holders, share-holders, etc.; store advertising; media advertising; and independent financial advisers. Little of the investment came via the independent advisers; most came from Marks and Spencer's own customers who were attracted by this fresh approach to marketing a unit trust and were impressed that it was backed by the Marks and Spencer name.

In October 1989 Marks and Spencer took another step towards becoming a major provider of financial services when they broadened their product range by launching a personal equity plan (PEP) under the name Marks and Spencer Tax-Free Savings Plan. This allows customers to invest up to £2,400 each year, or up to £200 a month, in the new Marks and Spencer UK Selection Portfolio, a unit trust that will invest exclusively in the UK stock market. Any profits from these savings are retained free of all taxes. Once again this financial service was marketed primarily through the Marks and Spencer Chargecard holders, and it was targeted at those Marks and Spencer customers who were potentially first-time investors in PEPs and whose usual mode of savings was via a building society account, where tax was deducted at source from any investment earned. By mid-1990 some 20,000 M & S customers had taken out a Marks and Spencer PEP.

Thus, first of all by developing their own critical mass of in-house credit card-holders, then by encouraging them to remain active card users, Marks and Spencer have been able to build an accurate profile of the demographics of their card-holders and their spending patterns. This has then helped them to tailor their financial services offering to a known and receptive audience who are willing to trust the brand name of Marks and Spencer, no matter what the product they are selling. Worthington (1986) discusses this synergy of retailer credit cards and direct marketing in more depth, while Bliss (1988) even suggests that in the future retailers will seek to dominate the distribution channels for financial service products.

A further example of retailer behaviour of this sort can be found in Australia where Coles Myer, Australia's pre-eminent trading company, is seeking to gain dominance over the Australian banks in the provision of a payments system service.

RETAILERS AND EFTPOS IN AUSTRALIA

Twenty cents of each Australian retail dollar are spent with Coles Myer, which is the largest non-government employer in Australia with over 155,000 employees. The company's sales figures make it the twelfth largest retailer in the world and the third largest outside the United States. Through an associate company, Australian Retail Financial Networks, Coles Myer runs its own 'in-house' credit cards under its various trading names – Myer Stores, Grace Brothers, Target, etc. – as well as managing the credit card bases for other Australian retailers such as Country Road. With a total of 2.2 million credit card accounts, 1.5 million of which are active in that they have a recorded transaction within the last three months, Coles Myer is already a major player in the Australian plastic card industry. The two major department store groups within Coles Myer, Myer Stores and Grace Brothers, have respectively 107 million and 100 million credit card transactions per year, and this volume of throughput also makes the Coles Myer group a major player in the Australian payments systems industry. It is upon this platform that Coles Myer has begun to shape the retailer/supplier relationship in Australian plastic cards and payment systems.

The 'gateways'

The current interchange system covers both EFTPOS and ATM transactions and it is known as inter-bankability. It relies on 'gateways' – currently the four major banks with their in-house processing facilities, which operate on behalf of other parties, e.g. the credit unions, building societies or retailers – to facilitate the interchange of transactions. Figure 5.1 illustrates the current system.

The establishment of an interchange dependent on 'gateways' into the system has also led to some inter-compatibility between the systems of some of the major banks. Thus Westpac and the Commonwealth Bank, both of which are headquartered in Sydney, share a common ATM/EFTPOS system whereby card-holders from either bank can use their cards for transactions in equipment installed by either bank. A similar reciprocity exists between the ANZ and the NAB, the two Melbourne-headquartered banks, and it is these arrangements plus the availability of large numbers of ATMs in Australia per head of

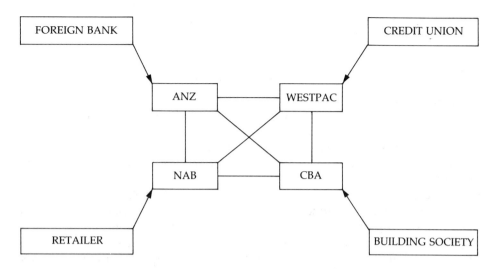

Figure 5.1 The 'gateway' system

population which make it such an interesting country to report on in terms of card ownership, usage and payment systems.

For a major retailer such as Coles Myer, the existing gateway system is disadvantageous, for to be tied to any one or even any pair of banks – for example, Westpac/Commonwealth or ANZ/NAB – would be to deny its customers who hold cards issued by the rival banks the ability to use those cards in EFTPOS terminals inside Coles Myer to purchase goods or services. Equally disadvantageous to Coles Myer is the fact that, at the end of the pilot schemes initiated by all the major banks interested in EFTPOS, the banks quite naturally wanted to charge Coles Myer for the terminals and for the transactions that took place through them. The banks would then charge each other fees for processing each other's transactions.

Coles Myer saw no reason why it should pay for either the terminals or the transactions that might have taken place through them. The pilot schemes were wound down and Coles Myer set about developing its own EFTPOS strategy which took into account what it as a retailer wanted from the system and not, as had previously been the case, what the banks wanted from an EFTPOS system. By 1986 Coles Myer had developed its position and it then issued a document to card issuers and payment systems operators requesting their proposals on how to create an EFTPOS system suited to the needs of Australia's leading retailer. The overriding criterion for assessing the alternatives put forward is that EFTPOS, if it is to be implemented by Coles Myer, must provide cost-effective enhancement of customer service and enable customer payment for goods and services using funds held with *all* card services providers.

The 'open' system

Coles Myer takes the view that, as the current Australian card issuers cannot present a unified system to the retailers through which *all* cards will be accepted and they insist on charging retailers for the transaction costs associated with the 'gateway' payment reconciliation system, then on to this confused and costly situation Coles Myer will impose the solution that suits it the best.

Coles Myer will therefore equip itself with the right sort of point-of-sale equipment to which a unified EFTPOS system can be added. This already exists in most of the Myer and Grace Brothers department stores and will be in the Super K-Mart food and non-food supermarkets by the end of 1992. The Target Discount chain and the food-only K-Mart supermarkets will also have decisions made about point-of-sale re-equipment by the end of 1992 – all with a view to adding EFTPOS equipment later. Coles Myer takes the view that any point-of-sale equipment installed will be owned by and under the direct control of Coles Myer.

Furthermore, Coles Myer sees no justification for paying transaction charges to enter the existing gateway system for access to the card issuers' clearing system for reconciling transactions. This is particularly so given the large volume of credit card transactions already being handled by Coles Myer and the consequent level of merchant service fee charge paid by Coles Myer, for what it considers to be an inefficient mechanism by which it receives the funds derived from card transactions. Consequently, Coles Myer intends to create a retailer-owned and -run transaction-processing service which will provide an 'open' service to those who are currently forced to enter the transaction-processing system via a gateway. They intend to implement a system which will enhance current credit card-processing facilities between Coles Myer and the relevant card service providers. The open system will (a) reduce the cost of processing credit card transactions, (b) result in a further reduction of the merchant service fee and (c) accelerate the receipt of funds derived from these transactions. Diagrammatically, the open system is shown in Figure 5.2.

Here transactions from all Coles Myer stores – plus transactions from other organisations which currently have to use one of the big four gateway banks – will be processed through the Coles Myer open system, and Coles Myer, having processed and reconciled these transactions, will then implement a switching system to forward these accumulated transaction values to the relevant card issuers. This will be done via entering the gateway system, probably via the National Australian Bank (NAB) of which Coles Myer is a corporate client. The NAB will, however, only be handling the sum totals of all

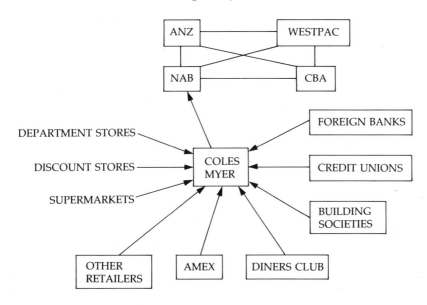

Figure 5.2 The 'open' system

transactions processed by Coles Myer and rerouting these debits or credits to the other card service providers represented by other gateway banks. Coles Myer would then naturally require a contribution from those card service providers towards the cost of this delivery service, just as now the gateway bank charges Coles Myer for its transaction services.

What we are seeing in Australia is a retailer seeking to gain dominance over suppliers in the provision of a payments system service. Once such a system is in place, Coles Myer will initiate staged enhancements to its current equipment and systems which will lead in the long term to the provision of a full EFTPOS service in the majority of its stores, through which it will be able to add value to its retail offerings. Of particular significance for retailer/supplier relationships in other countries with a large ownership and use of credit/debit cards is the rationale and the method by which Coles Myer in Australia has sought to move 'upstream' in the channel of distribution for payments systems. It has done this in order both to capture the extra added value from the processing of credit/debit transactions and to gain control of the channel so that it can dictate an EFTPOS implementation strategy that it believes is more appropriate for itself and its consumers. Research by Worthington (1990b) suggests that retailers in the United Kingdom are following similar strategies by collecting and sorting all card data from their stores and then charging the credit card companies for forwarding these, data to them.

CONCLUSIONS

Developments in the UK and other countries have shown how, by using their power in the distribution channel, retailers can outmanoeuvre the often more static banks to offer a wide range of financial services. These then pose a direct threat to the traditional providers of these financial services, for just as cost structures are forcing the banks, building societies, insurance companies, etc. to re-evaluate their distribution networks, so a new customer-friendly competitor is arriving on the scene, one whose distribution network is both extensive and well established.

Not only do retailers have power and presence in the distribution channel, but they are also, by the very nature of their business, close to their customers and well aware of their requirements, be they for goods or for services such as financial services. Retailers, particularly those with their own store cards, have become skilled practitioners at developing the relationship between retailer and customer, and as the demand for credit plateaus or even declines, these retailers will need to be imaginative in developing new relationships through their card offerings. These new relationships might well be based on areas of business such as financial services where the retailer's competitive advantage is the marketing database provided by its own cards. Suitably targeted cardholders can then be mailed and offered services such as personal loans and unit trusts, which currently have no truly effective distribution network and which retailers can offer with few effective distribution costs.

In the early 1980s, retailers discovered that they could narrow their focus by creating propositions aimed at specific customer segments. Now technology enables the segment size to be reduced to a single individual – the 'segment-of-one marketing'. This brings together two formerly independent concepts, information retrieval and service delivery, into a new working relationship. On the one side is a proprietary database of customer preferences and purchasing behaviour, and on the other side is a disciplined, tightly engineered approach to service delivery that uses the information base to tailor a service package for individual customers.

Increasingly, consumers are putting more value on being treated as individuals and they are demanding customised products and services delivered at the moment of need. They also value the reassurance and stability that comes from an enduring relationship with somebody who understands, and can respond to, their specific needs. Retailers have both the ability and the aptitude to respond to these consumer demands and increasingly they are using financial services as the vehicle through which to develop the retailer–customer relationship.

Roger Hymas, managing director of Burton Group Financial Services, has stated that they see themselves as major players in the UK financial services industry and that they are using their database system to build individual profiles of their customers from which individual propositions are made to them through personalised communication, in the form of store card statement mailing packs, solus mailing, telemarketing or even sales force leads.

Retailers, however, need to be aware that entry into the financial services market is not a licence to print money and also that they need to pay attention to sustaining competitive advantage in their core businesses. Benetton provides an example of the constraints that can face retailers in entering the financial services market. Earlier in this chapter, reference was made to Benetton's alliance with the Prudential Corporation; but as we have seen, by February 1990 Benetton had sold its stake in this joint insurance venture and was retreating from the financial services arena. The reason given was that Benetton had decided to concentrate its capital investment on the group's core activities and that it could not sustain its financial services developments when revenues from its clothing business were failing to match historical growth levels.

Such reverses do not mean that retailers' interest in financial services is merely a passing fad. Those retailers with secure core businesses will still be looking for new income streams, and with their experience of and empathy towards the end consumer they are in a strong position to compete effectively with the traditional specialists in the provision of financial services. Such competition may not be across the board – retailers' interests are focused in the personal rather than the corporate sector, for instance – and except for companies such as Marks and Spencer, it may be limited by the consumer's perception of the advantages and probity of 'specialist' financial service providers. However, while retail strategies will continue to be characterised by both success and failure, there seems little doubt that their presence in the market is likely to persist and will itself have implications for the behaviour of the specialist provider.

Chapter 6

IT and financial services in the USA

Philip Dover

The business environment is increasingly characterised by turbulence, resulting in sudden reassessments of the growth prospects of entire industries as well as dramatic upheavals in the relative positions of firms within an industry. The causes of such turbulence are both numerous and interdependent, but it is by now apparent that a major engine of the unprecedented instability is technology or, more precisely, the emergence of rapidly changing technologies in the environment. Nowhere has this been more evident than in the financial services industry where computing and information technology have not only revolutionised 'back-office' activity such as data processing and management support and decision making, but also, more importantly, have impacted the 'front-office' delivery system through the provision of a variety of electronic funds transfer (EFT) products. Retail products such as automatic teller machines (ATMs), point-of-sale (POS) debit cards and in-home computerised banking are increasingly available in both western Europe and the United States, as are electronic systems for cash management, foreign exchange transactions and merchant banking for corporate clients.

This chapter will focus on the US experience of developing and diffusing strategic innovations in retail financial services. Particular emphasis will be placed on the myriad approaches taken to home banking. Managerial lessons will be sought that can be applied to future EFT implementation.

RETAIL BANKING IN THE UNITED STATES

Due to past regulatory restrictions on inter-state banking, most US bank branch networks were local or regional in extent. However, growing deregulation has eliminated legal constraints on price competition for most products, with a consequent substantial decline in most product margins. Similarly, there have been product extensions (e.g., insurance and mutual funds) that allow banks to cross-sell aggressively in order to encourage customers to consolidate balances with their primary banks. Consequently, many large US banks have begun building larger distribution systems through acquisitions, thus gaining advantage over smaller competitors in both unit costs and marketing effectiveness. Consolidation has also been accelerated by the collapse of the savings and loan industry and the fiscal problems of a number of commercial banks.* But it must be pointed out that developing and implementing highly integrated product lines, marketing support systems and service functions across branch networks and different geographic locations is no simple task. Thus it is felt that, although the small US banks will increasingly feel strong pressure from larger competitors, the US banking scene will remain somewhat fragmented for the near future (see, for instance, Kimball and Gregor, 1989). It is within this environment that we must evaluate technological innovations in the retail financial sector.

ATMs

New York's Chemical Bank placed the first Docutel unit in operation in 1969. Current overall consumer market penetration of ATM cards stands at about 60 per cent of all households (Haisten, 1991). However, further penetration will be more difficult as much of the market portion remaining without ATM cards is inveterately opposed to them. Over half of the non-user group say 'nothing could get me to use them [ATMs]' (Lederman, 1989).

Other data show that activity rates – the portion of the card-holder base that actually uses the card in an average month – now average slightly over 50 per cent. The overall average usage rate among ATM users is just over six monthly cash withdrawals, which is higher than the average number of monthly branch visits (4.75) among consumers overall. Withdrawals are the only type of ATM transaction with virtually universal acceptance among ATM users. The next most common type of ATM transaction – deposits – are engaged in by just over 50 per cent of ATM users. ATM-offering institutions report, on average, that 61 per cent of their overall transaction volume is comprised of cash withdrawals, while only about 10 per cent is accounted for by deposits. The psychological objections to making a deposit in an ATM are fairly clear (mistrust of system reliability, fear that deposits might disappear, and uncertainty about funds availability).

Further penetration and usage of ATMs would seem to depend largely on a number of factors. First is the imaginative extension of product services and

---

*Size, of course, does not guarantee immunity from failure. The Bank of New England, one of the top 20 US banks, declared insolvency in 1992.

locales. While almost all larger banks now offer automatic teller machines in their branch offices, a growing number of banks have built substantial networks of off-site ATMs. Banks are increasingly installing the machines on-site at office complexes for the use of corporate employees, at shopping malls and supermarkets, in hospitals, post offices and sporting arenas. Similarly, new banking and non-banking applications that may increase ATM usage are point-of-sale debit transactions, interim statements, payroll cheque, deposits with cash back, and the ability to dispense traveller's cheques and postage stamps. As an executive of Union Trust in Stamford, Connecticut, noted: 'Our overall corporate strategy is to provide our customers with as many opportunities to use self-service banking as much as they can' (Jaben, 1987).

Secondly, an important facilitating feature that will further encourage the use of ATMs is the growth of networks that banks join on both a regional and national basis. The principal role of shared-network participation is extension of locational convenience for customers. For example, two automated banking networks in Kansas recently joined forces to make virtually all cash machines in the state available to customers. The interchange agreement will give more than a million debit and credit card-holders access to about 350 automated teller machines in some 175 financial institutions. Similarly, Bay Banks, a Massachusetts company that has made a heavy strategic commitment to ATMs, has just announced a policy of accepting 'others-on-us' transactions from any ATM card-holder in the United States. The benefits of networking can also be seen in cost reduction for banks. The president of the New York Cash Exchange (NYCE), a switch processor for an ATM network, observed that 'Once your ATMs are pumping transactions at a rapid rate, they are 50 percent to 75 percent cheaper than teller transactions' (Jaben, 1987).

This leads to an interesting dilemma currently faced by ATM managers. The traditional cost justification was that ATMs were economically rational because they displaced bricks and mortar and tellers. A more recent claim is that the rationale for ATMs needs to come from increasing revenue. Fundamentally, the debate stems from the ambivalent status of ATMs. Are they a product or a delivery system? If they are a product, then a provider of ATM service can ill afford to give very much of it away free. On the other hand, ATMs have become an expected extension of the delivery system, like branches. As it would hardly be possible to charge people for account access *per se* at branches, it is a difficult task to justify charging for account access via ATMs. Despite this, increased attention is being focused on pricing ATM services as a potential means of improving banks' financial performance. Four different types of ATM pricing receive most consideration:

- Periodic (monthly or annual) card fees.
- 'Us-on-us' transaction fees (i.e. use of own bank ATM).
- 'Us-on-others' transaction fees (i.e. use of other bank ATM).
- No fees at all.

Currently, only 6 per cent of top bank and thrift offerers of ATM service charge monthly or annual ATM card fees. Only about one in five (22 per cent) of ATM-offering top banks and thrifts charge their customers transaction fees for use of proprietary ATMs (us-on-us). Moreover, most (over 80 per cent) of these will waive these fees on the basis of account balances, relationships or other conditions. Fees for interchanged transactions at others' terminals are the most common type of ATM fee levied. Over 60 per cent presently charge such fees.

Some institutions report successful price initiatives, while others report problems. For example, on average, banks record not insignificant card base loss of customers (over 10 per cent) resulting from implementation of monthly or annual card fees. Moreover, loss of ATM transactions is only the tip of an iceberg representing a far greater risk. This is the problem of customer or account disenfranchisement. Decisions on such issues as ATM pricing and distribution, therefore, should not be viewed in isolation but as part of the banks' integrated product portfolio.

POINT OF SALE (POS)

Increasingly, banks are repositioning their ATM cards as debit cards. These cards offer the value-added benefit of being accepted at the point of sale where consumers can pay for retail purchases at merchant terminals which immediately debit the consumer's account and credit the merchant's. Although early over-optimistic forecasts were not realised, leading debit card issuers have reported dramatic gains in card-holder and debit card activity over the past year (Cohen, 1991). It is interesting to reflect on the short but chequered history of this new technology.

It has not been easy for banks to develop a strategy to convince a customer to use what appears, at first glance, to be a floatless credit card. Moreover, regional networks have many ATM users but relatively few retail establishments in which to use them. Merchants have been reluctant to handle debit card transactions due to the cost of debit POS installation and the merchant discount applied to each transaction that covers the cost of handling the transaction. This latter was found offensive to many merchants as they viewed the debit card as an alternative to writing cheques rather than using bank cards.

In 1987 MasterCard and Visa announced the impending introduction of a nationally available debit card called Entree. They stated: 'We believe that Entree will galvanize the banking industry around a single POS debit product that will help move EFT to the next plateau.' That is, the card would prove a rallying point by finally providing a single set of standards nationwide. The product worked by placing a portable logo or bug on ATM cards which allowed them to be used both for ATMs and POS. Entree was intended to be an on-line funds transfer system, debiting the card-holder's account instantaneously. If there were insufficient funds in the account, the transaction would not go through. Entree attracted about 200 participating banks before it was permanently dismantled in late 1990 by an anti-trust suit brought against the card associations by 14 state attorneys-general. The suit alleged that the Entree programme would be an anti-competitive monolith that would harm smaller debit programmes.

Bankers were not happy with this decision. It was seen to slow down national POS development and the move towards defining a set of rules and standards. It did, however, reflect a US mindframe. As J. Paul Boushelle of the American Banking Association noted: 'In this country, whenever anybody says they're going to do something nationally, there's the charge that it smacks of collusion' (*ABA Banking Journal*, 1990).

It is increasingly appreciated, however, that Entree would have saved both consumers and banks a great deal of bother concerning the linking of different networks. The Entree mark would have said: 'Look for this one mark anywhere in the country.' As a result, a dozen of the largest regional automated teller machines networks are discussing the start-up of a national debit card system that would allow consumers to deduct purchases instantly from their chequing accounts. The system, which would use ATM access cards for identification, would charge customers a transaction fee while the merchant would incur only the cost of installing the terminals. The network systems, which operate more than 80 per cent of the regional ATMs in the country, hope to have the debit card network operational by late 1992. Similarly, MasterCard and Visa have both continued to pursue the debit card market with their individual programmes – Master Debit and Visa Debit. With these programmes, banks offering ATM cards have either the MasterCard or Visa logo on their cards, thus giving them extended POS capability at merchants that accept bank cards. Payments are automatically debited from the card-holder's chequing account, as opposed to being posted to a monthly credit card statement.

Debit cards have been part of the banking scene for 20 years or so without gaining much customer or merchant acceptance. There are two major reasons why bankers *now* feel that the concept of debit cards is alive and well. First, the growth of network systems has aided adoption. For example, Master Debit and Visa Debit programmes have helped expand the merchant acceptance of debit cards – all stores that accept MasterCard and Visa bank cards will also accept their debit cards. On the other hand, debit cards issued without the MasterCard or Visa affiliation have received less favourable merchant response throughout the country. Secondly, banks have been able to develop an increasingly realistic approach to customer segmentation. The debit card is *not* for everyone, but will be of major convenience to those who pay with cash or a cheque. There are about 30 per cent of consumers who do *not* like to use credit cards for whom the debit card can fill a gap. Even for those who hold credit cards, there are some who do not like to use up the availability of their credit line, and they like the discipline of not having the purchases going against a credit balance that can build up. To date, for the most part, grocery stores and gas stations are the leaders in terms of debit card acceptance. It is here that most cheques are written. Increasingly, debit cards are no longer seen as a challenge to other cards. Customers and merchants alike are able to distinguish the complementary roles of debit and credit cards.

As with ATMs, the issue of pricing has arisen with debit cards. Should customers be charged a fee for the 'privilege' of using the card? Norwest Electronic Delivery Service of Minneapolis, for example, in introducing its Visa Debit programme chose to charge a monthly fee of $1.75 for the card. The longer-term customer reactions to such a move remain to be seen.

IN-HOME BANKING

It is in the area of home banking that both the opportunities and the problems of technology application are most vividly illustrated. Already a number of banks have offered screen-based home-banking systems – that is, where consumers interface with their bank through home computers – and failed. It has been estimated that, by the end of 1988, there were only about 100,000 consumer subscribers to home banking and about half that number of business users. What went wrong and what is the current status of home banking? First, if a bank wishes to provide remote banking, it must wrestle with the choice of technology selection for provision of the delivery mechanism. Uncertainty about which will emerge as the dominant technology, for which markets and which uses, has made many bankers take a 'wait and see' approach to new product adoption. Let us take a look at the available technologies.

Stand-alone screen-based systems

A number of banks, including all the major money centre banks in New York – Chase, Chemical, Manufacturers Hanover, Citibank – have invested heavily in developing software for their own, stand-alone home-banking systems. Here the home computer is used as the terminal to provide such services as funds transfer between accounts, account balance determination, loan instigation and bill paying. The experience of Chemical Bank in offering its Pronto home-banking service is fairly typical. It is estimated that Chemical, along with its partner AT & T, spent about $70 million on developing and marketing the Pronto system. It hoped not only to market the service to its own and competitors' customers in the New York area, but to license the technology to other banks across the country. The service was available at a flat charge of $12 a month, although users could obtain stock quotations for an additional per-minute charge. In late 1988 it was announced that Chemical was discontinuing its Pronto services 'because the market hadn't developed'. The bank advised an estimated 25,000 home-banking subscribers that their accounts would be cancelled. Many other banks have ceased their PC-based home-banking services or, like Chase Manhattan or Citicorp, have scaled down their services.

Many reasons have been postulated for product failure. These include the following:

- *Limited computer penetration.* Surveys show that the proportion of households that own personal computers has reached about 10 per cent, with only 3.3 million US homes equipped with both computers and modems. Moreover, many home-banking programs were compatible only with specific computer terminals, further limiting the potential market. This meant that consumers interested in accessing home banking often had to lease both software *and* hardware to operate the system. As one banking consultant noted: 'It appealed mainly to people that I call tech-heads, people fascinated by computers.' Certain systems (e.g. Bank of America) can be used with a TV set, although the cost of a keyboard ($300–350) is seen as a strong disincentive to consumer adoption. Consequently, the PC remains the delivery system of choice.
- *Limited services available.* Lack of consumer interest in home banking stems largely from the limited services provided. The stand-alone systems offer little beyond the home-banking services. Even the home-banking options proved restrictive and expensive for most home users. Pronto, for example, was unable to encourage many retailers to participate in the programme, leaving subscribers to pay a few of their bills electronically and the remainder by traditional, labour-intensive methods. The promised benefits of convenience were simply insufficient to overcome individual scepticism, suspicion and resistance to change.
- *Competing delivery systems.* Dedicated home-banking systems compete with home banking incorporated into broader videotex systems. Consumers (other banks as well as end users), fearing technological obsolescence and wasted investment, tend to wait for a single technology to emerge as dominant in a particular market. Such technological ascendancy may be some time in coming as new technologies continue to impact on home banking. For example, voice response vehicles offer an alternative to screen-based systems for delivering home-banking services (see below).
- *Optimistic forecasts.* At the time of Pronto's launch in late 1983, one industry study forecast that, by 1985, 250 banks would be providing home-banking services to 1,250,000 accounts, displacing 105 million paper-based transactions each year. Of course, such optimism was greatly misplaced. As has so often been the case, the forecasters were apparently enamoured of the product's technological merit (for an excellent review of forecasting errors see Schnaars and Berenson, 1986). They failed to consider many aspects of the markets they intended to serve. For example, was there a need for

in-home computerised banking? How many customers were there? What would the customers be willing to pay for it? Did the benefits justify the costs? The concept of in-home computerised banking has had nearly two decades of false starts. It has taken this period of time for most bankers to accept reluctantly that home banking cannot succeed if it is packaged as a stand-alone product.

Home banking as part of a videotex system

To date there have been hundreds of experiments in on-line information services in the USA. The database services geared to the professional users – Dow Jones News/Retrieval, Nexis, Lexis and others – have been more profitable than the consumer-oriented videotex services.[*] In fact, Europe is well ahead of the US market in general interest, consumer videotex systems. European countries and Japan have succeeded in developing uniform standards for videotex services, while the US market remains fragmented and better known for its costly failures than for its successes. For example, the Times-Mirror group spent $30 million in introducing Gateway while Knight-Ridder Newspapers invested over $50 million in developing and commercialising Viewtron. Banks and other financial services institutions such as Merrill Lynch were involved as partners in these and other experiments. Neither system drew more than a few thousand subscribers, insufficient to offset costs. Again both companies wrongly assumed that the consumer would willingly bear the cost of product development. In Knight-Ridder's case, the cost of the special terminal required to access the service was $600, making the price of admission too high (Diebold, 1988).

It is now generally agreed by bankers that electronic banking services need to be part of a broader home information service. Past failures have made many bankers take a 'wait and see' approach to home banking and no experiment is being more keenly watched than that of Prodigy. Prodigy Services is a joint venture of IBM and Sears that to date has invested about $650 million in developing a videotex system (Brown, 1991). It is anticipated that they will have invested $1 billion by the time Prodigy breaks even (Chakravarty and McGlinn, 1989).

To get Prodigy, subscribers must have a personal computer with an average amount of memory, a graphics card and a modem. A wide variety of services is provided, including airline reservations, home shopping, home banking and stock brokering. Furthermore, Prodigy is one of the few services to carry advertising. So far, some 170 companies, including American Express and J.C. Penney, have signed up to advertise. New subscribers pay $49.95 to gain the

---

[*]For the purpose of this article, videotex is defined as interactive (i.e. two-way) electronic information services that are low-cost and consumer-oriented, usually transmitted by telephone lines to home computers (Diebold, 1988).

system software, six individual passwords – for use by up to six members of the family – and three months of free use. After this time, subscribers pay a flat $12.95 a month. To date, 13 banks provide full-service home banking at a supplemental fee of $5–13 per month, depending on extent of service and regional price sensitivity. The participants include major banks, such as Wells Fargo, BankOne and Manufacturers Hanover.

Will it succeed? All told, there are about 9 million US households with computers compatible with Prodigy. It is estimated that Prodigy will require penetration of around 2.5 million homes to recover its investment. By mid-1991 more than 1 million members had signed up, with home banking reportedly one of the most popular services. The system's subscriber base has grown steadily and impressively as it has entered new regional markets and it is hoped to have at least 2 million subscribers within the next year. It is now the largest of the videotex systems, although it faces strong direct competition from Compuserve, a Columbus (Ohio) company owned by H & R Block and GEnie, a unit of General Electric. And, of course, the Japanese are not far behind. Nintendo Co., the Japanese manufacturer of a highly popular home entertainment system, has taken a first step towards creating a network that can deliver home shopping, banking and other financial services. It estimates that 20 million US households currently have its TV-based entertainment system. By developing a modem and controller to work with the entertainment console, Nintendo will provide an array of videotex offerings, including brokerage and home banking, to this captive audience.

There is an indication that bankers affiliated to the Prodigy system are taking a realistic but increasingly enthusiastic view of their opportunities. The Citizens & Southern National Bank in Atlanta started offering its HomeEc home-banking project late in 1988, in conjunction with Prodigy. Senior officers saw home banking as 'another way of doing business and we've got to be there at the right time', although they did not expect HomeEc to be a profitable venture for some time. Indeed, what is hoped for is the solidifying of relationships with existing customers as well as the growth of new customers. Talk is more in terms of banking relationships and cross-selling opportunities than it is about profit making. One bank that has high hopes for Prodigy is Manufacturers Hanover Trust. The New York bank started its own PC-based home banking service in 1985 but 'didn't set the world on fire'. By linking with Prodigy it feels it will 'give us a much broader product that will appeal to a larger base. It means a lot more marketing activity than we could provide for ourselves' (Tyson, 1989). Again the focus is on relationship banking. The bank's home-banking customers 'have more accounts and greater depths of funds with the accounts'. In fact, it is estimated that the average bank customer has 1.7 accounts, while a home-banking customer has between 4.7 and 5.7 accounts (Jaben, 1989). The Prodigy user profile conforms to this high net worth image. Average family income of subscribers is $70,000, while 29 per cent have postgraduate degrees. Similarly, Wells Fargo Bank, in announcing an exclusive deal with Prodigy in California, indicated: 'We're looking to reach PC owners for whom using a computer is just like using a VCR, a microwave oven, and an ATM.'

The potential videotex 'readership' is directly linked to the number of PCs installed in the home. Only a fraction of these currently have modems. But the price of computer equipment is steadily declining, and the growth of videotex services is creating a further demand for affordable terminals. Prodigy management expects that a true mass market will develop when the total price of a computer, modem and monitor drops below $500. Perhaps Prodigy will finally be the impetus for the future success of PC-based home banking. Certainly the *Wall Street Journal* appears excited. It has named Prodigy as one of the enterprises poised to lead business into the 1990s. However, many bankers remain sceptical, and certainly Prodigy must establish a good track record for the industry to recover from all the past failures.

Telephone banking

Banks seem to be increasingly turning to the telephone to bridge the gulf between the popularity of ATMs and the potential of personal computers. A growing number of banks are installing 'audiotex' or automated voice-response systems to take phone calls from customers. Customers call a special number, usually using a touch-tone phone, and a human-sounding voice instructs customers what numbers to push to get the information they seek. The services offer information on account balances, which cheques have cleared, and which deposits have been credited to the account. Some also offer rate information on bank products, and the ability to transfer funds between accounts.

Consumer demand has been considerably stronger for telephone banking than for videotex, its PC counterpart. An obvious reason for this is that most customers already have a touch-tone phone – all it requires to use a typical voice-response system. Less obviously, using the telephone demands less behavioural change than interfacing with a PC. It appears that the cost of equipment and 'technophobia' remain hurdles to computer-based home banking. Technophobia will not be overcome unless people can be shown that a system is 'non-threatening and simple' (Fink, 1989). Such difficulties are much less evident with telephone banking where early results are encouraging. For example, Citibank introduced its telephone banking service, CitiTouch, in June of 1988. By the end of the year it was receiving 400,000 calls a month, a number that was steadily rising. When Chemical pulled the plug on Pronto, its PC-based system, it replaced it with an automated telephone access system, ServiceXtra, that offers every feature provided by Pronto except electronic bill paying. Surveys suggest that customers want banking by phone. Currently, Chemical Bank receives over 1.3 million calls a month (handled by service reps or automated voice responses) and expects that to grow by 20 per cent a year.

Callers now opt for the automated service 30 per cent more often than a year previously. While a typical call involving a service rep lasts 2.5 minutes, an automated call lasts only 1.5 minutes and requires no labour cost. The net result has been a reduction in cost per call (*Communications News*, 1991).

As the undoubted technology leader in banking, Citibank continues to redefine the scope of electronic financial services available. Given that PCs and telephones offer competing ways to bring banking to the home, it was inevitable that someone would seek to incorporate the advantages of each technology. Enter Citicorp with the 'enhanced telephone', a hybrid device that can be described as a computerised telephone and looks like an overweight telephone with a small screen attached. Users have all the functions available to personal computer owners who conduct banking at home. The transaction data are shown on a cathode ray tube that can display 40 characters on 18 lines in a single screen. Most banking functions can be performed using the telephone keypad and the new phone is designed to become the primary phone in the household. Introduced in early 1991, the device sells for $49 plus a $10 monthly fee. As fast followers, Chase Manhattan and Manufacturers Hanover are planning similar product introductions. Conscious of the need to add value, the proposed Manufacturers device will also deliver advanced telephone services such as voice messaging and caller identification and information services like stock quotations. It is hoped that versions of the enhanced telephone (or their equivalent, such as AT & T's 'smart phone') will eventually have a slot for the insertion of a smart card. Once this feature is available, people will be able to do the ultimate in home banking: get 'cash' at home by transferring funds from their chequing account to the smart or debit card, which could then be used to make purchases in stores.

In fact, the one type of telephone banking that has not yet caught on is bill paying. Paying bills electronically is particularly complicated because customers must give a lot of information over the phone, including the amounts to be paid and who should receive the transfers. It is relatively costly and, without a large volume of customers signed up for the programme, it is difficult to justify on a strict accounting basis. It also raises once again the thorny question of whether or not to charge for the service as most other telephone banking services are provided free. Such problems are accentuated by the reluctance of merchants to accept electronic transfers. Merchants will only contemplate switching if they are assured of sufficient transaction volume. Larger banks are starting to work with merchants to assist them to develop electronic systems. Small banks too are looking to third-party networkers to provide the volume to permit a satisfactory return on processing. In its role as a switch station for several ATM networks in the Midwest, Fifth Third provides a voice-response system that includes bill paying. More than one-third of the 500 banks that participate in the networks have signed up for the audiotex. Thanks to the volume that results, the bank guarantees each bill payment (Fink, 1989).

Interestingly, the currently most innovative bill-paying system reverts back to PC application. The CheckFree service enables subscribers to use their PCs to direct payments to any merchant or individual from their accounts in any financial institution participating in the automated clearing house system. The big advantage of the system, therefore, is that it can pay *anyone*, compared with most home-banking services that pay only vendors registered with the bank to accept such payments. CheckFree issues payment either by electronic funds transfer through the Federal Reserve System to payees registered to receive such funds, or by paper cheque to individuals and businesses not registered. Subscribers pay a one-time $49 fee for a start-up kit that includes the software, a manual and the first month's usage. Thereafter, the service costs $9 a month for 20 payments, plus $3 a month for each additional 10 payments.

CheckFree has no affiliations with or obligations to any banks. It is a privately-held company, financed by its principals and five insurance companies as venture-capital investors. It is therefore offering banks the ability to provide a home-banking service without it costing the banks a penny. CheckFree also assumes the responsibility of interesting the merchant in receiving some sort of direct payment. This should prove an attractive alternative to banks grown wary of their own expensive and largely unsuccessful attempts at home, banking.

LESSONS LEARNED FROM THE US EXPERIENCE

The impact of technology has had a profound effect on the provision of retail financial services in the USA. Undoubtedly, this influence will both continue and accelerate. And yet electronic banking has not so far fulfilled its expectations. The product development experiences described in this chapter present management with guidelines for future strategic assessment of technological opportunities. Some of these ideas follow.

First, it is naïve to believe that radical technological innovations will quickly gain high levels of market penetration. Experience with ATMs revealed a slow consumer adoption process, but this analogue was ignored when POS and in-home banking products were introduced with wildly optimistic forecasts. There is a strong body of knowledge that suggests a number of powerful barriers exist to the early societal diffusion of an innovation (for application of the concept to banking see Dover, 1988). These include natural consumer conservatism, a reluctance to change behavioural patterns and an unwillingness to assume risk. Such concerns are exacerbated by the presence of technology which adds to the fear of the unknown and raises questions of obsolescence. As was recently observed: 'For a technology to affect the way we live, it has to be cheap, simple to use and offer a strong reason to use it. So far, for computer banking, those signposts are not there' (*Time,* 1990).

It is interesting to note that banks operating screen-based home-banking schemes have slowly become more realistic in their target marketing schemes. Having courted the consumer market and found it unresponsive, many banks are adapting their services to the needs of small businesses. 'Office banking' is seen as a useful cash management tool for the small business person who is sensitive to cash flow problems. Moreover, small business is becoming increasingly familiar with computers and has more of a need to know the status of its banking situation. There is still a future for home banking, but it will not be fully realised until the consumer's fear of technology has been overcome.

Along with shifts in segmentation, bankers appear to be changing their goals for electronic retail services. Initial objectives centred on cost containment and revenue enhancement. Now the theme most often sounded relates to investment for long-term customer loyalty and an emphasis on relationship banking. One banker sees home banking as 'another way of doing business and we've got to be there at the right time. Maybe in five to ten years a profit will result, but that doesn't seem to be a concern now' (Jaben, 1989).

Secondly, financial services executives must do a better job of matching technologies with market needs. Innovations such as stand-alone, screen-based home-banking systems show strong evidence of being largely technology-driven. Bankers, seeing the potential cost economies available from a successful, high-volume home-banking service, pushed development of the product without assessing likely market requirements or acceptability. Product failure came as an expensive surprise for reasons previously mentioned – low PC household penetration, limited banking services available, weak merchant support, and so on. Such failure should *not* have been a surprise given the myopic view of product-market appropriateness.

Here again a lesson can be learned from the activities of Citibank. For the past dozen years they have operated a 'lab' in the basement of a Manhattan office building to test the consumer-banking technology of the future. In the 1970s the lab helped give birth to the bank's automated teller machines. More recently it helped design Citibank's newest home-banking device, the enhanced telephone. Using one-way mirrors and video cameras, Citibank workers watch and record consumers' reaction to a device, then modify the technology accordingly.

Thirdly, the diffusion of technological innovation will be accelerated by the consolidation of services through networks or third-party providers. Volume usage necessary to recoup investment in a new service is substantial and acts as a deterrent to product development in many small or medium-sized organisations. Moreover, new technological ideas require significant initial consumer education which is often beyond the means of the individual bank. The successful, cost-effective application of technologies also requires highly skilled people. The growth of networks that provide electronic services (e.g. CIRRUS and NYCE for ATMs; Prodigy for videotex) makes products such as ATMs, POS and home banking accessible to a widening range of financial

institutions. Many of these networkers are not affiliated to financial organisations. As such, as well as absorbing many of the development costs, they do
not pose a direct competitive threat to financial service providers. A service like
CheckFree, for example, is not constrained by the banks used by payer or
payee. These third-party networks will also reduce the fragmentation that
pervades US banking as it gropes towards deregulation. Outsourcing, the
hiring of an outside firm to handle one or more automated functions within a
firm, increased by 16 per cent among banks in the USA in 1990 (Rector, 1991).

Finally, technological innovation will continue to act as an agent for change
in the financial services market. Its impact will also remain managerially
challenging. The constant introduction of new technology-based products will
greatly shorten the product life cycles of existing products. At the same time,
consumers faced with choosing products provided by alternative delivery
systems (e.g. screen-based vs voice-based home banking) will often defer
selection and slow the adoption process until a standard, dominant technology
emerges.

Other technologies are poised to enter the retail financial services industry.
In a few years, the technology of the Integrated Services Digital Network
(ISDN) will allow users to split a single telephone line into several voice and
data channels that can be used simultaneously. Cable poses an increasing
threat to traditional phone lines as a means of bringing data to the home, the
integration of PCs, TVs and POS into a unified home intelligence/entertain-
ment system grows closer, and branches seek to automate further through the
provision of platform-level PC intelligence to up-market service customers. For
example, Citicorp now claims that it can process a mortgage application in 15
minutes through enhanced automation. US banks are certainly intending to
invest more in technology. Expenditure on point-of-sale technology rose to
almost 3 per cent of investment expenditure in 1990, compared with about 1.5
per cent in 1987. Comparative figures for voice-response and home-banking
services were 8 per cent and 3 per cent respectively. Consultants at McKinsey
estimated that Citibank spent about $1.5 billion in 1988 on technology systems
from computers to telecommunications – about 13 per cent of the banking
industry's outlay.

Banks and other financial services in the USA face a challenging time.
Technology will play a pervasive and perverse role for the foreseeable future.
Investment in technology will be necessary if only for defensive purposes.
However, return on investment will require a longer-term perspective than has
previously been the case. In fact, banks must learn to treat technology as a key
strategic tool in the search for sustainable competitive advantage.

Chapter 7

The management of IT in financial services

Harry Scarbrough

Previous chapters have identified the product-market implications and management challenges posed by IT for the financial services sector. It is clear from this that IT does not have an independent impact upon organisations. Whether it is used well or badly depends upon the way in which it is managed. As IT becomes increasingly central to the competitive dynamics of financial services, the management of IT has strategic as well as operational consequences. This chapter will address the strategic management of IT and highlight the role which different levels of management play in integrating IT and business strategy.

DEFINITIONS

Although technology suppliers have a vested interest in turning IT into packages and products, treating the management of IT as simply a matter of which package to buy would be losing sight of two critical features of its organisational application.

The first is the importance of the organisational knowledge and architectures within which specific implementations of IT are developed. The performance and maintenance of even the most 'user-friendly' package are dependent upon the skills and operating structures within which it is located. In reviewing the management of IT, then, we need to consider technology in the broadest sense. As Figure 7.1 indicates, technology can be analysed as a hierarchy of different levels, extending from the detailed hardware and software of a specific implementation, through the overall systems design and architecture, up to the level of technological expertise, general models and assumptions. This view of technology indicates that the management of IT is a multi-faceted

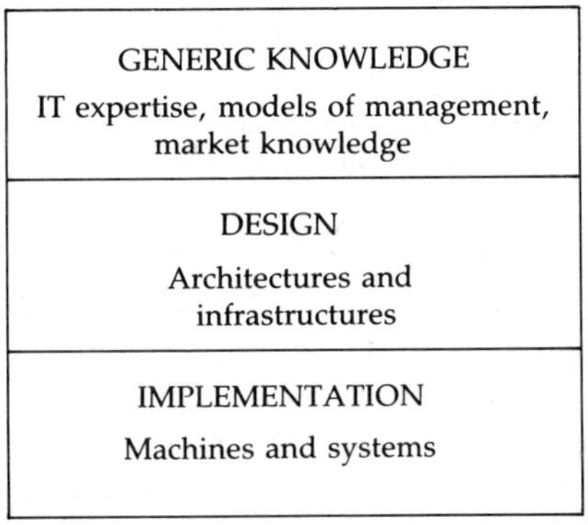

GENERIC KNOWLEDGE IT expertise, models of management, market knowledge
DESIGN Architectures and infrastructures
IMPLEMENTATION Machines and systems

Figure 7.1 Levels of technology

process that encompasses nurturing the right skills and structures, as much as deploying different kinds of hardware and software.

The second critical feature of IT is to do with its competitive impact. IT is an 'enabling technology': that is, in its hardware and software form it is highly flexible and can be readily applied to any task which is based on the processing of information. We have already noted how pervasive such a technology can be in financial services. However, the corollary of such ready availability is that IT packages have little intrinsic competitive value. It is the management of IT – the deployment of expertise, innovative applications to service delivery, and so on – which creates the unique product offering on which competitive advantage is based.

INTEGRATION OF IT AND BUSINESS STRATEGY

The financial services sector is seeing increasing pressures to integrate strategy and IT. The rationale for such integration can be defined in a multitude of ways: the sheer size and time-scale of IT expenditures, for instance, or the product-market opportunities created by IT. However, as indicated above, whatever the motives behind attempts to link IT to strategy, such integration demands careful attention to the organisational and market context in which IT is being applied.

Talk of integrating strategy and IT may be glib rhetoric unless both the technology and the organisation's strategy are meticulously analysed. The analysis of the technology, for instance, suggests that integration implies different things at different levels: new systems not only need to be technically linked into existing infrastructures, but must also be complemented by appropriate skills on the part of users and developers.

Equally important is the understanding of strategy itself. This term encompasses a variety of levels from product-market strategy through to business unit and corporate strategy. Given the diversified conglomerate structure of many financial institutions, it is the integration of IT at the business strategy level which is often the most important task.

Strategy can be understood as having both an inward- and an outward-facing aspect. Within the organisation, strategy provides a benchmark for the definition of functional goals and the pursuit of efficiency. In its outward-facing aspect, however, strategy is to do with the competitive posture of the firm and the distinctive value that it provides to the customer. These aspects are interrelated, of course, to the extent that the organisation's performance and efficiency affect its competitiveness in the marketplace. Similarly, IT can support both aspects of strategy by serving in some contexts as a means of achieving internal efficiency, and in others as a tool for creating competitive products and services. This is highlighted in Figure 7.2.

Applying the above analysis to financial services suggests that IT in the sector corresponds to a variety of forms, not all of them having strategic importance. In the 'back-office' or 'factory' context of payments processing, IT is crucial to the organisation's functioning, but has only an indirect impact upon customers. Equally, certain IT applications – the use of PCs by insurance salespeople, for example – may have high customer visibility but little to do with the day-to-day running of the business as a whole. Where IT is most strategic, however, is in those applications which have a pervasive effect both upon the workings of the organisation and upon the quality of service provided to customers. The development of customer databases and branch information systems seems to embody this kind of strategic significance.

As the various types of IT system identified above have quite different business implications, it follows that they should be managed differently. In particular, integrating IT with the inward- and outward-facing aspects of strategy leads to two different perspectives. The internal perspective highlights the fit between the information system (IS) needs of the organisation and IT-based systems. The kind of methodologies involved in achieving such a fit are described in Table 7.1, which outlines different approaches to the design of IS. The outward-facing dimension, on the other hand, is to do with exploiting the product-market possibilities of the technology. These market and competitive possibilities are centred on the value which IT systems can help to create for the customer through product differentiation and innovation (see Table 7.2).

In a competitive context, strategy is much more of a moving target. The industry structure itself may be changing, often under the influence of IT. Porter and Millar (1985) cite the effect which the development of information systems for real-estate brokers has had upon the marketing of mortgage packages in the USA. The ability to compare mortgages against one another has inevitably enhanced competition in that area. Such structural change might

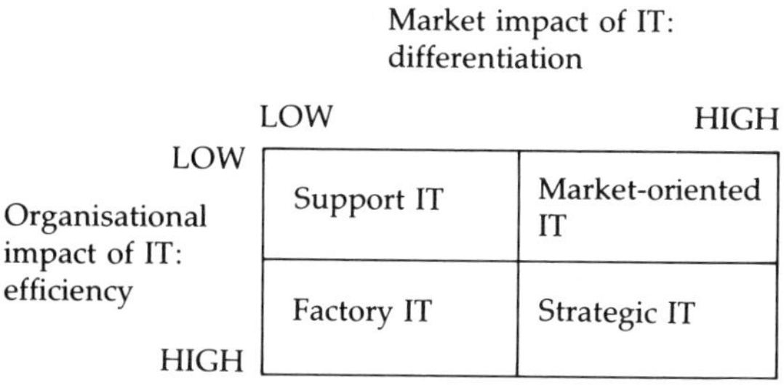

Market impact of IT:
differentiation

	LOW	HIGH
LOW	Support IT	Market-oriented IT
HIGH	Factory IT	Strategic IT

Organisational
impact of IT:
efficiency

Figure 7.2 Integration of IT and strategy

also involve the lowering of entry barriers to the industry, or a shift in the market power of different groups.

The competitive viewpoint suggests different ways of analysing technology. Rather than viewing systems in terms of their operational characteristics – contrasting batch processing with on-line real-time systems, for instance – the competitive viewpoint emphasises the effect which different levels of technology have on the customer. The core technology of hardware, systems software and related technical knowledge is largely provided by technology suppliers

Table 7.1 Strategic data-planning methodologies

- *Business systems planning (BSP).* Analysis of data flows within a company so that the origins and destination of data can be mapped on to organisation chart then simplified and rationalised. Top-down analysis of information sub-systems. On that basis hardware and software purchases are made. A mainly bottom-up planning process.

- *Critical success factors (CSFs).* Top managers specify the most critical parts of their responsibilities and the data they need to perform those tasks in the best way; this serves as a statement of necessary outputs for IT staff – data availability, speed of reporting, duplication, format of reports, etc. all made explicit.

- *The applications portfolio.* Answers questions on existing spread of IT through the company by creating a pyramid diagram of functions and their relative degree of automation. Important to monitor spread of IT so that spending priorities can be established and plans for centralised databases carried out.

- *Information engineering (Martin).* Focuses on data (vs software engineering's focus on design and programming of software). Given that the types of data employed in organisations do not change very much, these are taken as the starting point and broken down into entity types (customers, employees) and attributes. Use of data modelling. Data models become the foundation stone on which more variable computerised procedures are built.

- *The 'stages' approach (Nolan).* Sees attitudes to, control of and expenditure upon data processing as conforming to a life cycle of development. Helps to raise the right questions at the right time.

Source: Sinclair (1989).

Table 7.2 Competitive benefits of IT

Benefits	Examples
Product differentiation	Improve quality of customer service through branch information systems
	Greater product variety through use of expert systems
'Lock in' customers or distributors	Automated direct debits and standing orders
	Value-added networks for home banking or insurance intermediaries
Create new services	ATMs, corporate cash management, in-home banking

and has only indirect effects on customer service (Steiner and Teixeira, 1990). From a competitive standpoint, there is no incentive to seek innovations or leadership in this area. As long as the core technology is reliable and provides an adequate platform for other technologies, it has no competitive implications. This may help to explain the persistence of out-of-date languages, notably COBOL, in the programming and maintenance area of IT functions.

Applications technology, on the other hand, has a much greater visible impact on customer service. It is also much more specific to a particular organisation, demanding a wider mix of knowledge and skills to be developed and implemented. Consequently, the competitive potential of this technology is much greater.

This analysis highlights the need for the business integration of IT to encompass both the inward- and outward-facing aspects of strategy. Certainly, there is a need for formal analysis and co-ordination of IT developments with information system needs and organisational goals. However, it is equally important to recognise that such integration would be no more than tidy housekeeping if it were divorced from the application of IT to a changing and unpredictable market context. There may be a tendency to subordinate IT to rational analysis and an explicit hierarchy of strategic plans and objectives. This needs to be tempered by a recognition that market and competitive forces are ultimately irrational, and demand a degree of flexibility which formal planning alone cannot provide.

IT INTEGRATION: STRUCTURES AND PROCESSES

The integration of IT with strategy cannot be achieved through rhetoric or formal planning alone. This would be confusing the visible mechanisms through which managers think about strategy with its actual embodiment in a firm's product-market posture. Strategy is not a matter of rational planning alone, but also involves responsiveness to the marketplace. Mintzberg (1987), for instance, talks about the 'crafting' of strategy in this light. In addition, strategy is communicated and shaped by the organisation itself.

Organisation structures influence strategy through the political interests which they create (Miles and Snow, 1978). Powerful vested interests will help to shape the patterns of strategy commitments, and may promote or obstruct the strategic integration of IT. In turn, structure reflects the specialised skills and product offerings on which competitive advantage is based. Such core skills assume a particular importance in the design and delivery of complex financial products. They cannot be achieved overnight through top-down planning or management fiat.

In talking about the strategic integration of IT, then, we are talking about a complex set of relationships between the marketplace, the organisation itself and the processes of planning and strategy formulation. These relationships and the role of IT within them can be described as 'strategic leverage', the features of which are outlined below.

The leverage between IT integration and competition is a two-way process. Formal planning can help to achieve competitive advantage by levering the appropriate skills, products and delivery systems against competitors' offerings. Equally, by affecting a firm's competitive position, the forces of market and technological change can bring about changes in an organisation's strategy and structure. This can happen in two ways. The adoption of new IT-based systems, for example, may be the direct result of competitor impact on a firm's market share. Alternatively, it may reflect the more indirect absorption of new ideas and 'recipes' generated by competing firms. The widespread adoption of customer databases can be cited as a product of the latter factor, rather than a response to the technology's competitive impact.

This analysis suggests that the much-heralded integration of IT with corporate strategy can take place on a number of levels, and that not all forms of integration are necessarily critical to a firm's competitive performance.

- *Rhetorical*. Although top management statements about the strategic importance of IT may be dismissed as token gestures, in certain contexts the symbolic statements and actions of senior management do have an effect upon the use and development of IT. In the process of organisational change, for example, such 'management of meaning' (Pettigrew, 1987) may have an enormous effect upon the perceptions and actions of those middle

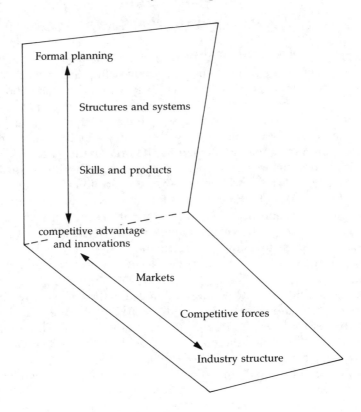

Figure 7.3 IT and strategic leverage

managers upon whom the success or failure of change programmes depends.

- *Formal*. The integration of IT with organisational goals may be achieved through the formal means of written plans and objectives. At this level, the integration of IT is expressed through the creation of explicit IT strategies which can be co-ordinated with the overall planning process of the firm. The scale and bureaucratic structures of financial institutions encourage this formalised aspect of integration. In a survey by Wilson (1989), 86 per cent of financial service firms, versus 73 per cent of the 500 largest UK companies, reported having an 'IS strategy'.

  The formal integration of IT depends upon strategy making being, in part at least, a formal exercise. In periods of change and uncertainty, however, there is a danger that formal planning mechanisms will generate 'paralysis by analysis' (Lenz and Lyles, 1985). There is also a danger that such formal devices will maximise the efficiency of the existing organisation, while neglecting the need for change in more fundamental areas such as culture and skills.

- *Political and structural*. Organisation structures generate political interests and boundaries which shape the formulation and implementation of strategy. Integration of IT and strategy at a political or structural level might come about in a variety of ways: through IS management seeking a career path into strategic management, for instance, or through new structural forms which reward innovative and entrepreneurial uses of IT.

  There is also the less desirable possibility that IT functions – sometimes in unholy alliance with technology suppliers – will use their influence to promote technology-driven strategies which fail to address competitive needs. In a study of the branch network plans of the UK clearing banks, Smith and Wield (1988) found that IT functions promoted technology-driven and cost-oriented branch systems which detracted from overall branch efficiency and quality of service.

- *Products and skills*. This level is to do with the delivery systems, skills and products which constitute the firm's interface with the market. This is the level at which long-term competitive advantage is achieved. An example might be the way in which the product specialisation of the building societies has given them significant cost advantages over the banks.

  The integration of IT at this level is crucial to sustained competitive advantages, but it also comes up against entrenched cultures and practices. It highlights the importance of the institutionalised division of labour in financial service firms. The existing skills within an organisation not only shape the quality and range of products that it offers, but also provide a template for the acquisition of new skills.

In financial services, the traditional dominance of bankers and actuaries in the managerial division of labour has inevitably shaped the way in which IT is used and the role of IT experts within the organisation. Relatively few senior managers have any practical knowledge of IT – less than 1 per cent according to some estimates – and this inevitably constrains the use of IT to pursue business opportunities. Not only IT is affected by this, of course; much the same applies to other areas of expertise such as marketing and retailing skills (Dalbey, 1986). The integration of IT encounters constraints in operational areas too, where the existing legacy of skills, practices and technological investments helps to shape the way in which new IT systems are used or abused.

This analysis highlights the integration of IT at different levels of the organisation. It shows that on its own the rhetorical and formal integration of IT may be ineffective in achieving competitive advantage unless it carries through to the level of skills, products and delivery systems. There is no direct or automatic relationship between what happens formally at senior management level and the kind of products and skills which make up the organisation's competitive profile in the marketplace.

At the very least, there is likely to be a time lag between formal planning and outcomes at product-market level. This is due to the time taken to move up various learning curves on skills acquisition and product development. But, as we note below, the formal planning process itself may be shaped by crises of performance at the competitive level, and there may need to be a degree of *organisational learning* from this competitive environment. The latter may be an important step in adapting formal decision-making processes to the exploitation of IT.

Very often, the formal integration of IT and strategy is blighted by a political and financial investment in existing structures, products and skills. These constraints on the full-scale integration of IT into competitive performance may necessitate extensive and long-term programmes of *change management* if they are to be fully overcome. Transforming practices, products and skills throughout the organisation involves changing structures and creating new political coalitions. Formal policies and strategies are more likely to reflect than to drive the political and cultural leadership involved in such a transformation.

A further influence on the relationship between formal strategies and operational skills and structures is the important role played by innovation in achieving competitive advantage. Structures and skills not only need to reflect existing strategic objectives, but must also provide the kind of space, incentives and organisational arrangements that will encourage the emergence of *innovation*.

The importance of innovation can be gauged in a variety of ways. Some product innovations succeed in achieving only a short-lived competitive edge, and have to be continuously developed and refined if they are not to be overtaken by competitor reaction. Similarly, technology-based innovations in financial services rarely have any proprietary or patent protection and need to be carefully timed and marketed for maximum impact. However, at critical points in the evolution of industrial sectors, 'strategic innovations' (Whipp and Clark, 1986) may emerge which help change the face of the whole sector. In the process, those organisations which are most adept at exploiting the strategic innovation may be able to achieve an irreversible competitive advantage over their rivals.

Strategic innovations link products and processes in new ways which are uniquely attractive to customers. As a result the existing marketplace is transformed and new competitive rules of the game are created which favour one organisation or type of organisation over all others. The classic example of strategic innovation is Henry Ford's creation of a mass market for cars by linking standardised product design to mechanised, mass-production techniques. Until the emergence of Japanese techniques in the 1980s, production processes in the car industry were dominated by Fordist methods and the competitive process favoured those firms which emulated the Fordist virtues of mass-production efficiency.

One feature of strategic innovations is that they are not based on technology alone. Rather, technology – in Ford's case, the assembly line – is used to support a complete package of work organisation, management and product marketing and design. It follows that the innovative use of IT in financial services is likely to be most successful where it is successfully linked to organisational and marketing innovations. Thus, the competitive benefits of customer databases, for example, will be achieved only by those organisations which link the technical features of such systems to redesigned branch layouts and new staff competences in customer relations. Only then are customers likely to be persuaded that such technology is part of a completely new form of financial service, and not simply an add-on to existing clerical procedures.

ORGANISATIONAL LEARNING

The importance of organisational and technological learning to the formation of strategy is increasingly being recognised. Strategy is not simply a question of rational analysis, but also a matter of facilitating the learning processes that allow adaptation and innovation within a changing environment. Strategy can be defined as an 'architecture that guides competence building' (Pralahad and Hamel, 1990, p. 91).

Organisational learning takes place on two levels. 'Single-loop learning' (Argyris, 1977) is when decisions are based on the perceived success or failure of a previous policy without questioning the underlying norms and criteria on which the original policy itself was based. Like the thermostat of a central heating system, a single feedback loop operates. Double-loop learning, however, is where outcomes lead an organisation to question not only the prevailing policy, but also the underlying norms and structures from which that policy derived. In a context of innovation and change, the latter kind of learning process is crucial.

The advent of ATMs in the late 1970s provided a perfect example of the importance of organisational learning. Many firms did not know how to react to this new technology. One estimate from the USA suggests that less than 10 per cent of banks fully understood the implications when they began their ATM programmes (Jaben, 1988). Although some banks saw them as a means of reducing labour costs through fewer tellers and shorter banking hours, the machine usage was never high enough for that. Consequently, their ATM networks simply evolved as a convenience service rather than a teller replacement. Other banks saw them as a kind of loss-leader, but neglected to track whether they were effective in that role. Finally, another group installed ATMs simply as a defensive imitation of their competitors.

The case example of the Bank of Scotland demonstrates how these initial problems with the management of ATMs helped to stimulate an organisational learning process. This provided a platform for some clear thinking on the strategic use of IT.

CASE EXAMPLE: BANK OF SCOTLAND

The Bank of Scotland was one of the pioneers of computer technology in the UK, installing an IBM mainframe as far back as 1961. By the mid-1970s the growth of specialisation in the Bank's management of computer technology meant that systems tasks were devolved to two separate divisions: Computer Services and Management Services.

While this demarcation reflected the historical development of skills and experience in computer technology, it also created a duplication of activity, and, worse, served to institutionalise differences in perception between the two divisions. With each division locked into its own functional concerns, technical and financial criteria took precedence over the strategic or marketing dimensions of IT.

This narrowness of view was dramatically discredited with the advent of ATMs in the late 1970s. The two technical divisions simply could not see the new technology's potential marketing or service benefits. Instead, they focused on conventional operating criteria: projections of a poor return on investment when compared to the ATM's labour-saving effects.

But when a number of other banks, particularly the Royal Bank of Scotland, embraced ATMs as a major delivery system and began to attract customers with them, the Bank of Scotland was forced to review its 'wait and see' stance on this new technology. A reconstituted working party now decided that ATMs could indeed be cost-justified, and an extensive programme of installations was begun. Within a few years, the Bank's own efforts and its membership of ATM consortia put it on a par with its competitors in the deployment of this technology.

However, this was not the end of the story. Senior managers within the Bank viewed the ATM episode as a lesson on the need to change entrenched attitudes. A reappraisal of the Bank's approach to managing technology was initiated. This led first, in 1982, to the formation of a small Automation Planning department which was to act as a catalyst in generating a broader view of technological opportunities available to the Bank. The papers produced by this group helped to highlight the need for some basic structural change in the computing and systems area. Within a couple of years, the Management Services and Computer Services divisions had been merged and placed under the direction of the head of the original Automation Planning team.

Together with the appointment of a new treasurer and general manager, these organisational changes greatly enhanced the Bank's strategic awareness of the opportunities created by IT. This new-found awareness rapidly began to bear fruit in the shape of a collaborative venture with the Nottingham Building Society — 'Homelink'. This was the first home-banking product to be offered to retail customers in the UK, and it helped to establish the Bank as an important player in the field. Most important, it offered the Bank a means of entry into the lucrative south of England market without the cost of an elaborate and expensive bricks and mortar infrastructure. Although the new system was based on the Prestel viewdata system, and therefore was not attractive to large groups of personal customers, the Bank felt it offered a way forward for small to medium-sized businesses, and in 1985 launched its own product — HOBS (Home and Office Banking System) — targeted at exactly this market.

Although the experience of pioneers in the home-banking field has not always been a happy one – the Bank of Scotland has been notably reluctant to release figures on the number of HOBS customers – the home-banking innovation needs to be judged in the context of an overall shift in Bank policy. From a tardy and defensive response to ATMs, the Bank has moved towards being one of the most active users and developers of IT systems. This has borne fruit not only in terms of a variety of other technology-based products, but also in terms of enhancing UK-wide customer and industry perceptions of the bank.

Source: Scarbrough and Lannon (1989).

The adaptation of decision-making processes is particularly important in the financial appraisal of IT-based innovations. The problems of quantifying the qualitative marketing benefits of new IT delivery systems demand a less dogmatic application of return on investment techniques. In one sample of telecoms-based IS projects aimed explicitly at achieving competitive advantage, no less than 80 per cent had only been pushed through by ignoring or circumventing IS planning and project selection procedures (Earl and Runge, 1987). Although such projects can get through the system either on the basis of a sketchy financial justification or simply by being buried in other parts of the IT budget, it may be important to incorporate non-quantitative criteria such as competitive parity and customer pressure in their evaluation.

THE MANAGEMENT OF CHANGE

IT acts as both a stimulus to organisational change and an element in managing that change. The need for change may arise, as we noted earlier, from external competitive forces in which technology plays an important part.

Research by the Centre for Corporate Strategy and Change at the University of Warwick has helped to establish the role played by IT as one of a series of 'triggers' to change at a strategic level, and the range of issues which may be involved in managing that change (see Table 7.3). Despite increasing levels of uncertainty, much change in the sector involves planned programmes in which technology and organisational forms are developed together.

An important current example of simultaneous technological and organisational change is the rising importance of centralised IT-based services compared to standard branch networks. The transfer of all customer information to data networks threatens major changes in branches, eliminating layers of clerical work. A similar transformation may be expected too in the nature of the branch manager's work as decision support systems of the kind described in Chapter 4 come to be widely used. Figure 7.4 outlines the changing

Table 7.3 The management of change in the Big Four clearing banks and the building societies

Trigger	Issues
(a) The Big Four clearing banks	
Technology	Number of employees; industrial relations, manpower planning, general management, careers
Segmentation of branches	Dual-career structure, specialisation in work roles, job satisfaction, in-service professional education, equal opportunities, management development process, segmentalised bank culture
Emphasis on customer service	Cultural orientation, work roles, mass training
Profitability	Reward structures, appraisal, part-time employment
(b) The building societies	
Rapid growth	Management training, career planning, graduate recruitment, organisation structure
Rising costs	Performance appraisal, part-time employment
New services	Skills and systems, branch manager roles
Mergers	Staff rationalisation, industrial relations, general management

Source: Hendry (1987).

distribution of work tasks among a sample of 90 bank branch managers after the introduction of a credit scoring system.

A similar shift from procedural to more customer-oriented skills is visible in many insurance companies, again facilitated by the automation of clerical tasks and the provision of customer information through database technology. In this context, structural and cultural change may accompany the spread of IT, as Table 7.4 illustrates.

IT AND INNOVATION

The problem with managing innovation is that it is rarely amenable to formal planning. Much innovation arises accidentally or is stimulated by interaction between a firm and its customers. An example of the former is provided by a UK insurance company which linked an extensive group of independent agents to its mainframe computers simply to overcome the inadequacy of the

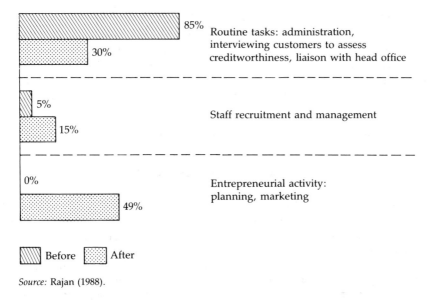

85% Routine tasks: administration, interviewing customers to assess creditworthiness, liaison with head office

30%

5% Staff recruitment and management

15%

0% Entrepreneurial activity: planning, marketing

49%

▨ Before   ▦ After

Source: Rajan (1988).

Figure 7.4 Impact of a credit scoring system on branch managers

Table 7.4 Cultural change in a mutual insurance company

	'Old culture'	*'New culture'*
Main tasks	Administration	Business development
Promotion	Seniority	Based on merit
Skills	Professional managers: administrative skills	Business management: strategic and commercial skills
Recruitment	'Grow your own'	External recruits from specialist areas
Structure	Hierarchical	Flatter management structure
Appraisal system	Loyalty and conformity	Performance-based

Source: Adapted from Watkins and Bryce (1989).

postal service in transmitting enquiries and policy information. Only later did it emerge that the ability to provide on-line quotes and premium information might be a competitive advantage (Earl *et al.*, 1988). Meanwhile, the importance of customer feedback is exemplified by a UK bank whose adoption of electronic banking was prompted in large part by the demands of its corporate customers.

To the extent that formal policies affect innovation at all, they need to be linked to structural and cultural change which encourages individual and group creativity. One such context is the entrepreneurial drive unleashed when a small group identifies a market or technological opportunity which can be pursued through innovation. A classic example of such an innovation is provided by the formation of the Direct Line insurance company, as shown in the case example.

CASE EXAMPLE:
DIRECT LINE INSURANCE COMPANY

As of 1991, the Direct Line insurance company employs 520 people distributed between its head office in Croydon and regional centres for England, Scotland and the north of England. Its product range encompasses motor, household and accident and sickness policies.

Direct Line was formed just six years ago by a group of four senior managers, led by Peter Wood, who broke away from an established insurance-broking firm. This group had formulated an innovative idea for an insurance company that would both underwrite and market policies directly to the public. Although other firms had developed phone selling of insurance, they had been acting simply as the telesales function for a group of conventional underwriting firms.

The group's business idea was not only dependent on an innovative use of IT, but could only have come from managers with an intimate awareness of both the insurance business and the potential of IT. It was no coincidence that all four were highly computer-literate — three of them having worked on IBM Systems programming.

In 1985 the group succeeded in linking up with the Royal Bank of Scotland and this helped them secure capital investment, access to an established customer base and regulatory approval.

SYSTEMS DEVELOPMENT

The new systems had to be developed in-house, and against a tight nine-month deadline set by the Royal Bank. The aim was 'To develop a computer system which would give insurance quotations, issue policy documentation, perform policy maintenance, issue renewals, electronically collect premiums and process claims. Furthermore, provide on-line marketing, advertising, underwriting and financial statistics.'

At the strategic level, the idea of selling insurance policies direct to the public had to be translated into systems which would maximise data capture over the phone — no personal contact through local branches or intermediaries here — while making relatively few demands of the potential customer. From a marketing point of view, the cost advantages of Direct Line had to be reinforced and not counterbalanced by its relative convenience to the customer. So one of the objectives of systems development was the simple notion that customers should not have to quote long, complicated policy or quotation numbers if they wanted to follow up an initial enquiry or make a claim.

These objectives demanded a highly flexible customer-oriented *database* as the means of storing and accessing information. This also provided a vehicle for the marketing of services. Even phone enquiries which were not converted into policies could provide a vital marketing resource. The data gathered provided a massive information base for the direct mailing of Direct Line products on a targeted basis.

Being competitive also meant a highly flexible system for rate setting. By developing systems structured around data and not having to reprint documentation for brokers, Direct Line would be able to adjust rates on a daily basis, compared with up to five or six months for conventional firms. This meant monitoring conversion rates for particular car model types – that is, the ratio of phone enquiries to policies sold – and adjusting rates accordingly.

Compared to the software, the hardware element in the technology was much less significant. Direct Line began operations with a £150,000 second-hand IBM mainframe plus a printer (though it has since graduated to a £2 million system).

THE MANAGEMENT OF EXPERTISE

The company attributes its successful system developments to:

1. The commitment of senior management to prudent technological innovation.
2. The calibre of its computer specialists.
3. Integration of executive management skills which combine financial, marketing, underwriting and computing expertise.

All of these factors are to do with expertise rather than technology. Direct Line is not driven by IT. Much emphasis is placed on having the right blend of skills within the company, the business itself being the product of a particular blend of IT, business and insurance skills.

But there is little point in having multi-skilled senior managers if the rest of the organisation is rigidly specialised and compartmentalised. In the IT area specifically, the IT director, Mike Flaherty, has stressed the need for business awareness, flexibility and user responsiveness among the 51 staff in his department.

Business awareness

- All new entrants to the IT function are required to spend at least a couple of days on the phone lines to give them the awareness that even a technically trivial task may have business implications.
- Many recruits into the IT area are mature people from Training Opportunities Scheme (TOPS) courses.

Flexibility

- IT staff work in multi-disciplinary project teams responsible for both development and maintenance rather than being sectioned off into development and processing functions.
- There was a conscious decision not to charge or do timesheets for the IT function.

User responsiveness

- Large projects are monitored by cross-functional working parties.
- To avoid responding passively to user demands, or creating a queue of projects, an executive committee of top managers carries out an active prioritisation of IT projects. This eliminates the kind of unnecessary and trivial IT work which a more passive prioritisation system can generate.

STRATEGY

The firm's competitive strategy used IT and the telephone system, together with a mixture of advertising and direct mailing, to eliminate the need for extensive networks of branches and intermediaries. As a result, the company could offer a highly responsive service at a much reduced cost: premium rates 20 per cent below most of their competitors. A whole range of technologies was involved in making this centralised IT resource accessible, cost-effective and attractive to the general public:

- The *phone system* and the advantages of computerised exchanges provided both a communications channel and a basis for the human interface with the customer.
- The use of *laser printers* to issue individual policies ensured a speedy follow-up to a phone conversation and a tangible form of security for the customer.
- By accepting only credit card and direct debit payments, the company streamlined its *payment systems* and handled all payments electronically. The accounts function for a premium income of £70 million could be managed by a staff of six.

The critical success factors for competitive success shifted from a firm's branch/intermediary network to factors such as media advertising spend, quality of telephone service and so on. Direct Line placed a high priority on closely monitoring key features of its telephone service: notably, tele-operators' manner, and the speed with which calls are handled — two and a half minutes' turnaround for a quick quote, and only seven minutes to arrange a complete policy. Management also paid close attention to the availability of insurance experience (sometimes overriding the computer) and factors such as regional accents and local knowledge. The latter was one of the reasons for the establishment of regional centres.

Careful attention to factors such as these helped Direct Line to achieve a retention rate of 86 per cent of customers on renewal — against an industry average of around 66 per cent — and a conversion rate of 1 in 5.

Although it is too early in the company's life to evaluate its long-run performance, there can be little doubt that its IT-based competitive strategy has been a convincing success in the first few years of its existence. It has achieved a customer base of 250,000 car drivers and 70,000 homeowners. Its most recent financial figures show an £8m profit. It has achieved an operating ratio (loss and expense ratio combined) of 95 per cent, one of the lowest in the UK, and is almost unique in making a profit on its underwriting activities.

Direct Line is a perfect illustration of a company exploiting an IT innovation to break down barriers to entry. It is also, like case of the Bank of Scotland, an instance of a relatively compact management structure providing an effective vehicle for the development of IT-based innovation. However, for the structural reasons noted earlier, innovations in the sector are still more likely to emerge from the large-scale and long-established institutions which continue to dominate the sector. Even Direct Line required the support of one such institution to gain access to the business.

It follows that a major problem for the management of innovation is developing it from within the bureaucratic context of large financial institutions. This means it is likely to involve breaking down departmental barriers and creating wider involvement in the development of new products and systems. History has shown that competitive benefits are derived from innovations which embody a unique combination of technological and service characteristics. It follows that the advantages of functional specialisation need to be tempered by cross-functional linkages. Multi-disciplinary project teams, for example, not only allow for the pooling of technical and business knowledge, but also create the kind of personal drive and commitment to innovation which is needed to overcome bureaucratic inertia.

A recent survey (Earl *et al.*, 1988) of competitively-oriented IT innovations found that 'formalised planning, rigorous control of information systems activities and investment in sophisticated strategic analysis methods' (p. 16) did little to contribute to the nurturing of innovation. Instead, the following factors were seen as crucial:

- *A new relationship between users and IT experts*: user management taking the lead in identifying business opportunities for IT systems, and IT activities being devolved to user groups.
- *Informal structures for identifying strategic innovations*: user teams and business units able to develop a more experimental approach to IT, using a range of the latest technologies and being aware of competitor developments and market needs.
- *The importance of project champions in promoting innovation projects and overcoming organisational resistance.*

Clearly, the kind of structural change implied by these factors may be difficult to achieve. There are fundamental constraints on the devolution of IT activities, as we note later, due to the distribution of IT expertise and the importance of central IT infrastructures in financial services. Similarly, it may be difficult to create the appropriate organisational climate for IT and product innovation outside of the existing functional structures. High-technology firms are able to establish innovation project teams whose activities can be distanced geographically and politically from the inertia of the mainstream organisation. Thus IBM created its PC by establishing a project group located outside of the existing structures and the prevailing mindset. However, in financial services, the dependence of any new product or system upon the existing infrastructures of branch networks and core technology tends to favour the dominant role of the existing functional expertise. Even where innovations are provided by outside suppliers, the organisational interface shaping their efforts is likely to be provided by IT specialists with functional responsibilities for existing systems.

MANAGING THE IT FUNCTION

Such factors make it all the more important that the IT function be appropriately organised so as to foster innovation as well as efficiency. However, the tensions between these twin imperatives are starting to take their toll of existing IT structures as well as senior IT personnel. Symptomatic of the kind of restructuring which IT functions are undergoing are recent developments at Barclays. Here a highly critical report from a US consultancy firm led to the adoption of a new strategy for IT – Automated Centralised Operations. This has resulted in 20 or more top IT managers losing their jobs and many more IT staff, especially on the computer operations side, being threatened with job losses.

The management of the IT function has also caused concern at the Midland Bank. In 1986 Midland set itself a target of reducing its cost–income ratio to the mid-60s by the end of decade, but the ratio actually rose to 76.5 per cent in 1990. This was despite a planned £1 billion investment in IT which aimed at achieving £200 million of cost savings.

The possibility for disappointing returns from IT investments is an ever-present problem in financial services, particularly because, as we noted earlier, so much investment is needed simply to stay in the payment systems game. However, as the above examples illustrate, the current emphasis on the competitive use of IT is creating a new set of demands which existing IT structures can hardly accommodate.

This can be seen at a number of levels. In terms of planning, for instance, the time-scale and size of IT spending demands sophisticated planning yet is dogged by various forms of uncertainty:

- The tendency for large IT projects to change in scope and purpose as they proceed.
- Variations in the medium- and long-term demand for products.
- The pressure on profit margins and variations in interest rates.
- Shortage of IT skills in the labour market.

Given the tendency for large IT projects to run out of control – around 70 per cent of UK computer projects over £0.5 million (*Financial Times*, 24.5.1991,

p. 12) – achieving efficiency in the use of IT is difficult enough. But when the innovative and effective use of IT is taken into consideration, an even broader range of problems – and possible changes – appears. These cluster around three broad issues: IT structures; the sourcing of IT expertise; and the relationship between users, customers and hybrids.

IT structures

Although the management of competitive innovations is arguably at the forefront of immediate concerns for the use of IT, the IT structures within many firms are often not designed for such tasks. They are the result of a lengthy process of evolution, lasting 20 years or more. Unlike, say, the car industry which originated in a product innovation, the pattern of computing technology in financial services corresponds to a 'reverse product cycle' (Barras, 1986). In other words, as Table 7.5 demonstrates, the application of this technology began in process areas such as transaction-processing systems, payroll and funds management, and only later extended into the areas of product quality and product innovation.

The significance of this cycle for IT structures is twofold. First, IT functions have developed an elaborate and specialised division of labour. Secondly, IT – or more accurately DP (data processing) – skills and perceptions have tended to focus on the parameters of process efficiency rather than on product quality or innovation.

The cultural constraints associated with the IT function's evolution may help to explain moves towards the reorganisation of IT activities. Such reorganisation may be prompted by technical factors such as the availability of more distributed forms of IT. It may also arise, as we noted in the Bank of Scotland case, from general dissatisfaction with the quality of service and decision making of the IT function.

Table 7.5 Reverse product cycle in financial services

Conventional product cycle	Reverse product cycle	Examples	
		Banking	Insurance
Product innovation	Process efficiency	Payments processing	Computerised policy records
Product quality	Product quality	Branch info systems	On-line quotations
Process efficiency	Product innovation	ATMs, home banking	Complete on-line service

Reorganisation of IT does not take place in a vacuum, of course. Some of the same structural factors which have shaped the existing IT function – and contributed to the ground swell of dissatisfaction – may continue to dog any reorganised form. It has been found, for instance, that the characteristics of the host organisation and its 'IS heritage' – that is, the history of IT within the organisation – exert a persistent influence upon IT structures (Feeny *et al.*, 1989).

Such factors are particularly important for financial services firms. In earlier chapters we noted that their strategies and structures were heavily conditioned by the nature of the financial service product and the infrastructures of branches and IT systems through which it is delivered. These structural elements have not only prevented firms from developing product-based structures such as product divisions, but by the same token have encouraged the kind of functional plus holding company structures in which IT activities are currently embedded.

Thus, although the reorganisation of IT can take a variety of structural forms – the major options are outlined in Table 7.6 – radical change in the IT area is likely to be dependent upon a strategic reorientation of the business as a whole. Structural change *per se* may be less important than the new kinds of accountability and user relations that it allows.

Equally, each structural option has its own advantages and disadvantages. In accounting terms, for instance, cost centres and budgeting may encourage a conservative approach to IT use. Yet, a profit centre relationship may demand costly mechanisms to control and price IT services, and may institutionalise an undesirably arm's-length relationship.

It is the latter option, nevertheless, which has been gaining ground as a means of controlling IT. Barclays Computer Operations, for example, has been

Table 7.6 Structural options for the IT function

- *Corporate service.* IT function a unified service reporting to corporate management. All forms of IT including distributed systems and PCs under the control of the central function.

- *Internal bureau.* IT centralised but run as a business, and reports like other business units. It charges other business units for its services.

- *Business venture.* IT business seeks revenue from outside host organisation through external marketing of products and services.

- *Decentralised.* IT a distributed function, where each business unit has its own IT capability or employs external suppliers. No central IT unit except for support of HQ functions.

- *Federal.* In addition to the IT groups within each business, a central IT function reporting to corporate management has responsibility for policy and architecture across the organisation.

Source: Feeny, *et al.* (1989).

established as a quasi-company and a profit centre in its own right. Although its main focus is on work for Barclays, it also bids for work outside the bank.

The development of such an arrangement has a good deal to do with the relationship that it fosters between users and IT experts. In particular, it involves defining the user as a customer. This has advantages for both sides. Bruce Hotter, BCO's managing director, expressed the IT function's view in the following terms:

> One of the big problems I have had as a monopoly is that my [internal] clients don't perceive that they're getting value for money – they think they may be getting ripped off . . . If you tell them you've got to reduce your cost base but, by the way, you're locked in to the Barclays IT department, they'll just say what do you expect me to do about it. (*Financial Times*, 18.4.91)

Other organisations such as National Westminster and Citibank have found this kind of relationship desirable, and the following advantages have been identified:

- The customer is responsible for its use of IT and is better able to identify innovation opportunities and allocate the costs of IT in the light of business performance.
- The morale of management and staff in the IT function is raised, as they are no longer burdened with the ambiguous task of balancing local against corporate IT needs, or rationing IT resources.
- The IT function is more flexible and user-responsive.
- The performance of the IT function is more visible.

The logic of users becoming customers is that a functional relationship is turned into a market or quasi-market relationship. Such a strategy therefore raises broader questions about the in- or out-sourcing of IT expertise and technology.

SOURCING OF IT EXPERTISE

IT development in financial services has always involved a mix of internal and external expertise and technology. The core technology of processing systems and mainframes has come from major suppliers such as IBM. Similarly, in the area of teleprocessing systems IBM's CICS and IMS packages are standard purchases. On the other hand, the maintenance of such core technologies, and the development of applications around them, has been largely a matter for the in-house IT function.

The balance seems to be determined to a significant extent by the relative efficiency and reliability of in-house versus out-sourced services for particular tasks. Also, the nature of the task itself is important. How easily can it be specified in advance and therefore regulated by a formal contract? Does it have implications for competitiveness or security?

Table 7.7 below outlines the critical features of internal and external supply and the kind of IT tasks for which each is most appropriate. To a large extent, these options are mutually supportive rather than mutually exclusive. Across a wide range of IT developments, there are significant advantages to be derived from a mix of internal and external expertise. For example, the standardisation of IT tasks creates greater potential for the use of packages. Since the latter spread their costs over a wide market and are marketed in a competitive context, they provide an efficient means of carrying out certain functions. On the other hand, the effective choice, contract specification and customisation of such a package may require an element of in-house expertise. Similarly, while innovative IT applications may depend upon organisationally specific and unique knowledge, they may also benefit from the specialist or industry-wide knowledge possessed by an external supplier.

Technological change inevitably shifts the distribution of IT tasks over time, as certain functions become standardised and other tasks become modularised. Thus, at one end of the scale, functions which are not visible to the customer and have limited competitive implications can be hived off to external suppliers, allowing the ruthless pursuit of maximum efficiency. The spread of 'facilities management' contracts seems to reflect this logic. Meanwhile, at the other end, the increasing adoption of IT-based product innovations which can be readily added on to existing core systems is helping to generate another important market for external suppliers. Finally, there are certain functionally interdependent tasks which are becoming increasingly important as IT spreads throughout the organisation. Tasks such as the central monitoring of computing standards and the integration of IT systems demand a combination of technical expertise and detailed organisational knowledge. They effectively guarantee a role for an in-house IT function for some time to come.

Table 7.7 Internal and external sourcing of IT expertise

In-house function	*External supplier*
(a) Features	
Organisation-specific knowledge	Generic/industry knowledge
Hierarchical control	Contractual control
Internal monopoly	Competitive market
(b) Appropriate tasks	
Frequently occurring tasks	Specifiable and easily evaluated tasks
Unpredictable and uncertain tasks	Standardised tasks
Functionally interdependent tasks	Independent tasks

Some managers see external supply contracts as the means of overcoming the perennial problems of meeting deadlines and achieving quality standards. Certainly, they do provide a market discipline which is difficult to achieve within hierarchical arrangements. They also provide a means of coping with the tension between the management of innovation and the pursuit of efficiency in the IT area.

Equally, however, reliance on a particular external supplier may create a dependency relationship which is just as constraining as the internal arrangements for IT. The problems which many firms have in adjusting their relationship with IBM is one example of this.

USERS, CUSTOMERS AND HYBRIDS

Whatever structural arrangements are forged between IT expertise and internal customers, there are clearly powerful incentives for the customer's role to be enhanced. However, turning a user into an effective customer is not simply a matter of providing the customer with financial leverage over the IT experts. It also involves a programme of IT education, such that the customer is expert enough to be able to identify and specify IT requirements. This was apparent when Citibank in the USA developed its user 'DIY' approach to IT and abolished its systems analysis department. The ability of users to manage their own projects through to completion was dependent less on the back-up of contract programmers than on a careful selection policy and hundreds of preparatory training courses in managing technology (Willcocks and Mason, 1987).

A related possibility is that user-friendly systems and fourth-generation languages (4GLs) will create a new division of labour between users and IT staff; one in which the user is much more in control of IT, and the IT expert's role becomes much more narrowly defined. As Doug Williams, Chase Manhattan's manager for European operations and systems, puts it:

> We won't need an interpreter in a few years. Most people will be computer literate. Instead of being systems analysts we will teach the business people how to run the system. We will take out a whole middle layer. We will end up with 'supertechies' who know the internal workings of the machines, but a whole layer of specialists/analysts will disappear. (*The Banker*, January 1990, p. 11)

The logic of this approach to user education may eventually lead to the development of 'hybrid managers'. These have been defined by the British Computer Society (BCS) as individuals possessing the following repertoire of skills:

- Technological competence: a knowledge base that allows the manager to recognise an IT opportunity, scale its size and complexity, and perhaps prototype it.

- Business confidence: experience and knowledge of a specific business area, such that IT application opportunities can be identified, justified and integrated into existing operations.
- Organisational skills: knowing how to get support from the IT function, and how to initiate an idea, as well as having the social and political skills to make things happen in consequence.

The BCS has proposed a large-scale training programme aimed at producing 10,000 hybrids by 1995. Organisations such as Esso have been early proponents of this approach; half of their top IT management have come in from line jobs. The effect, they claim, is that 75 per cent of their IT projects are now completed on time and within budget compared to 60 per cent in the past.

But while the advantages of hybrid managers are reinforced by the cultural divide which still exists between IT staff and mainstream management, that divide also makes their emergence much less likely. Organisations need to address the restructuring of departmental boundaries, the creation of possibilities for job rotation, and perhaps ultimately the career paths of both IT and mainstream managers if greater hybridity is to be achieved.

CONCLUSIONS

This chapter has consolidated our review of the management challenge posed by IT in financial services. The combination of changing technology and uncertain markets makes this a strategic challenge for many organisations. However, the undoubted need for IT to be integrated into business strategy must take account of the various levels at which integration can be prosecuted, and some of the underlying constraints on that integration. Formal plans and policies are only one element in exploiting IT for competitive purposes. Equally important, if not more so, are programmes of change management and the processes of learning and innovation out of which effective strategies emerge.

Notes on the contributors

Dr Harry Scarbrough (Editor) is Lecturer in Industrial Relations and Organisational Behaviour at Warwick Business School, University of Warwick. He is co-author with J. M. Corbett of *Technology and Organization* (Routledge, 1992), and is currently involved in a research project investigating Strategic Innovations in the Financial Services Sector. The latter is funded by the Joint Committee of the Economic and Social Research Council and the Science and Engineering Research Council.

Dr Philip A. Dover is Faculty Director of the International MBA at Babson College, Wellesley, Massachusetts, USA. He has researched and written on the application of IT in financial services in both a British and an American context.

Dr Rob Procter is Lecturer in Computer Science at the University of Edinburgh and is currently involved in the above-mentioned research project on Strategic Innovations in the Financial Services Sector, as well as the ESRC's PICT (Programme for Information and Communication Technology).

Steve Worthington was formerly Lecturer in Business Strategy at the University of Stirling, where he was the author of a series of influential reports and articles on the evolution of card payment systems in financial services. Until recently, he was Head of Marketing and Planning at the Co-operative Bank in Manchester.

Bibliography

ABA Banking Journal (1990) 'Entree is dead . . . long live debit cards!', September, pp. 109–12.

Argyris, C. (1977) 'Double loop learning in organizations', *Harvard Business Review*, September–October, pp. 115–25.

Barras, R. (1986) 'Towards a theory of innovation in services', *Research Policy*, vol. 15, pp. 161–73.

Bliss, M. (1988) 'The impact of retailers on financial services', *Long Range Planning*, vol. 21, no. 1, pp. 55–8.

Brown, P. B. (1991) 'On screen sales', *Inc.*, January, pp. 108–9.

Burke, T. (1989) *Retailer Plastic: Own label credit cards – a new competitive weapon in the High Street*, Working Paper No. 38, Polytechnic of Central London.

Carter, R. L., Chiplin, B., and Lewis, M. K. (1986) *Personal Financial Markets*, Oxford: Philip Allan.

Chakravarty, S. N., and McGlinn, E. (1989) 'This thing has to change people's habits', *Forbes*, 26 June, pp. 118–22.

Cohen, H. (1991) 'Debit cards start to make their move as surprise banking product of the '90s', *Bank Marketing*, March, pp. 22–5.

Communications News (1991) 'How Chemical Bank cuts costs, predicts call patterns', May, p. 10.

Dalbey, H. (1986) 'Planning on both sides of the Atlantic', *The Banker's Magazine*, March–April, pp. 33–46.

Diebold, J. (1988) 'Videotex in the US: an assessment', *Telecommunications*, July, pp. 79–83.

Dover, P. (1988) 'The effect of technology selection on consumer adoption of in-home computerised banking', *International Journal of Bank Marketing*, vol. 6, no. 2, pp. 31–7.

Earl, M. (1989) *Management Strategies for Information Technology*, London: Prentice Hall.

Earl, M. J., Feeny, D., Lockett, M., and Runge, D. (1988) 'Competitive advantage through information technology: eight maxims for senior managers', *Multinational Business*, Summer, pp. 15–21.

Earl, M. J., and Runge, D. A. (1987) *Using Telecommunications-based Information Systems for Competitive Advantage*, Research and Discussion Paper 87/1, Oxford: Oxford Institute of Information Management, Templeton College.

112

Feeny, D., Earl, M., and Edwards, B. (1989) *IS Arrangements to Suit Complex Organizations: An effective IS structure*, Research and Discussion Paper 89/4, Oxford: Oxford Institute of Information Management, Templeton College.

Feeny, D., and Knott, P. (1988) *IT and Marketing in the UK Life Insurance Industry*, Oxford: Oxford Institute of Information Management, Templeton College.

Fink, R. B. (1989) 'The phone or a PC?', *United States Banker*, May, p. 55.

Freyenfeld, W. (1984) *Decision Support Systems*, Manchester: NCC.

Friedman, A., and Cornford, D. (1989) *Computer Systems Development: History, organisation and implementation*, London: Wiley Information Systems.

Gershuny, J. (1978) *After Industrial Society?: The emerging self-service economy*, London: Macmillan.

Grossberg, S. (1988) *Neural Networks and Natural Intelligence*, Cambridge, Mass.: MIT Press.

Haisten, M. (1991) 'The ATM outlook', *Credit Union Management*, March, pp. 11–14.

Hendry, C. (1987) *Strategic Change and Human Resource Management in Retail Banking and Financial Services: An overview*, University of Warwick: Centre for Corporate Strategy and Change.

Howcroft, J. B., and Lavis, J. (1986) *Retail Banking: The new revolution in strategy and structure*, Oxford: Basil Blackwell.

Howcroft, J. B., and Lavis, J. (1987) 'Evolution of the payment system of London clearing banks', *Service Industries Journal*, vol. 7, no. 2, pp. 176–94.

Jaben, J. (1988) 'Banking on the phone', *United States Banker*, November, pp. 18–22.

Jaben, J. (1989) 'Can home banking rise from the ashes?', *Bankers Monthly*, May, pp. 50–5.

Kimball, R. C., and Gregor, W. T. (1989) 'Emerging distribution strategies in US retail banking', *Journal of Retail Banking*, Winter, pp. 4–16.

Klein, M., and Methlie, L. (1990) *Expert Systems: A decision support approach*, New York: Addison-Wesley.

Lederman, C. J. (1989) 'ATM strategies: looking ahead', *Journal of Retail Banking*, Winter, pp. 17–25.

Lenz, R. T., and Lyles, M. A. (1985) 'Paralysis by analysis: Is your planning system becoming too rational', *Long Range Planning*, vol. 18, no. 4, pp. 64–72.

Miles, R. E., and Snow, C. C. (1978) *Organizational Strategy, Structure and Process*, New York: McGraw-Hill.

Mintzberg, H. (1987) 'Crafting strategy', *Harvard Business Review*, July–August, pp. 66–75.

Monopolies and Mergers Commission (1989) *Credit Card Services*, London: HMSO.

Moran, M. (1991) *The Politics of the Financial Services Revolution*, London: Macmillan.

Pettigrew, A. M. (1987) 'Context and action in the transformation of the firm', *Journal of Management Studies*, vol. 24, no. 6, pp. 649–70.

Pollock, A. J. (1985) 'Banking: time to unbundle the services?', *Long Range Planning*, vol. 18, no. 1, pp. 36–41.

Porter, M. E. (1980) *Competitive Strategy*, New York: Free Press.

Porter, M. E., and Millar, V. (1985) 'How information gives you competitive advantage', *Harvard Business Review*, July–August, pp. 149–60.

Pralahad, C. K., and Hamel, G. (1990) 'The core competence of the corporation', *Harvard Business Review*, May–June, pp. 79–91.

Rajan, A. (1988) *Information Technology and Managers*, Institute for Manpower Studies Report No. 146.

Rector, T. L. (1991) 'Maximizing manpower', *Mortgage Banking*, February, pp. 27–30.

Rogers, E. M. (1962) *Diffusion of Innovations*, New York: Free Press.

Roth, A. B., and Van Der Velde, M. (1989) 'Investing in retail delivery system technology', *Journal of Retail Banking*, Summer, pp. 23–34.

Scarbrough, H., and Corbett, J. M. (1992) *Technology and Organization: Power, meaning and design*, London: Routledge.

Scarbrough, H., and Lannon, R. (1989) 'The management of innovation in the financial services sector: a case study', *Journal of Marketing Management*, vol. 5, no. 1, pp. 51–62.

Schnaars, S. P., and Berenson, C. (1986) 'Growth market forecasting revisited: a look back at a look forward', *California Management Review*, Summer, pp. 71–88.

Shamoon, S. (1989) 'From fabrics to finance', *The Banker*, February, pp. 20–6.

Shillito, D. (ed.) (1988) *Information Technology: A strategic guide for the UK insurance industry*, London: IBC Financial Technology.

Sinclair, S. W. (1989) 'Information technology and strategy revisited', *Multinational Business*, no. 4, pp. 8–15.

Smith, S., and Wield, D. (1988) 'New technology and bank work: banking on IT as an "organizational technology"', in L. Harris (ed.), *New Perspectives on the Financial System*, Beckenham: Croom Helm.

Steiner, T. D., and Teixeira, D. B. (1990) *Technology in Banking: Creating value and destroying profits*, Homewood, Ill: Business One Irwin.

Time (1990) 'Back to the velvet-roped lines', 9 January, p. 49.

Touche Ross International (1985) *The Impact of Technology in Banking*, TRI.

Tyson, D. O. (1989) 'Prodigy home banking arriving in New York City', *American Banker*, 18 April, p. 18.

Watkins, J., and Bryce, V. (1989) *The Management Development Dimension: Information technology in insurance*, Bristol: Bristol Business School.

Watkins, T. (1988) 'Developing trends in the marketing of life insurance', *Journal of Marketing Management*, vol. 4, no. 1, pp. 71–87.

Wells, G. E. (1989) 'The revolution in building societies', *Long Range Planning*, vol. 22, no. 5, pp. 30–7.

Whipp, R., and Clark, P. A. (1986) *Innovation and the Auto Industry: Product, process and work organization*, London: Frances Pinter.

Willcocks, L., and Mason, D. (1987) *Computerising Work: People, systems design and workplace relations*, London: Paradigm Press.

Wilson, T. D. (1989) 'The implementation of information system strategies in UK companies: aims and barriers to success', *International Journal of Information Management*, vol. 9, pp. 245–58.

Worthington, S. (1986) 'Retailer credit cards and direct marketing: a question of synergy', *Journal of Marketing Management*, vol. 2, no. 2, pp. 125–31.

Worthington, S. (1988) 'Credit cards in the United Kingdom: where the power lies in the battle between the banks and the retailers', *Journal of Marketing Management*, vol. 4, no. 1, pp. 61–70.

Worthington, S. (1990a) 'Retailer credit cards: A competitive threat', *International Journal of Bank Marketing*, vol. 8, no. 4, pp. 3–9.

Worthington, S. (1990b) 'The future for plastic cards and payment systems in the United Kingdom', University of Stirling.

Index